MAKING
MULTI-TRACK
MUSIC

JOHN PEEL

First published in Great Britain in 1994 by Making Music Ltd,
20 Bowling Green Lane, London EC1R 0BD

ISBN 1 872601 24 3

Printed and bound in Great Britain by Spottiswoode Ballantyne

Publisher: Adrian Walker

Edited by Jon Lewin

Design & additional editing by Tony Mitchell

Cover design by Sean McAlorum

Additional material by Paul Quinn, Steve Wright

Origination by Stirling Graphics

Distributed by International Music Publications Ltd

CONTENTS

HELLO

This book is a successor to our popular *Making Four-Track Music* handbook, which ran to four editions.

The reason for the change is simple. When we published the original book back in the mid-1980s, four-track was the affordable norm for the home recordist (at least for all but the lucky few). But the great strides in technology since then have introduced much greater sophistication not only to semi-pro recording gear, but also to the ideas and demands of musicians themselves.

The aim of *Making Multi-track Music* is thus to reflect the full potential of today's home studio.

Then again, you might still be pondering the purchase of your first four-track machine – in which case, welcome: start at *A Quick Tour* for your step-by-step guide.

If you're upgrading your system, whether for personal enjoyment or commercial reasons (small studios have proliferated since the late eighties), skip ahead a few pages and you'll find plenty of insights and sound advice.

New digital formats and budget 24-tracks are among the topics now included, as is the ever-expanding role played by MIDI and computers (although for a comprehensive explanation of MIDI sequencing, you should read this book in conjunction with our *Making Music With Computers & Software* manual).

Whatever your preferred style of music or method of recording, *Making Multi-track Music* will help you choose the right hardware for your needs (and budget), and then help you make the best possible recordings using it. From first principles to advanced studio techniques, emphasis is on hands-on practicalities rather than cold academic theory. Tech-talk is kept to a user-friendly minimum.

Written by an experienced sound recordist, the book aims to show that it's really no more work to put together an excellent production than a mediocre one; and also that engineering and production can be just as fascinating, creative and rewarding a part of the musical process as songwriting and performance.

Have fun...

A QUICK TOUR

(AND A LITTLE TECH-TALK)

This is the place to start if you're completely new to the world of recording music – by the same token, if you already know your way round the general principles, you'll maybe want to skip to the next chapter. Later on, I'll introduce the few technical terms that it's really useful to know something about, but we'll begin with the kind of questions that first-time buyers most commonly ask retailers...

WHAT IS MULTI-TRACK?

It matters not whether we're talking about a four-track cassette recorder or a 48-track pro studio, the principles are exactly the same. And the fundamental name of the game is: flexibility. The original method of recording was to stick a microphone in front of a live performance and tape the whole thing onto a mono (or in later times, stereo) recorder. Why don't we still do it that way? Well, say someone makes a mistake. Then we have to go back and record everything again. Or, assuming everybody's performances are fine, we decide on playback that the vocals need to be a little louder in the mix. Again, we have to start over. And this time, maybe the guitarist fluffs it. Yup, record yet again. This can get seriously frustrating. And, even when everything is fine, we might want our arrangement to have two lead guitar parts, but we've only got one lead guitarist. Problems.

Ignoring for the moment the practical restrictions imposed by, say, a four-track set-up, the basic idea of multi-track is to give each instrument its own tape track. Now we can record the performance just as before, but when somebody cocks it up, we don't have to scrap everybody else's efforts – we just record the one bodged part again. We can do this because it's on its own track, and our miscreant muso can listen to all the other recorded tracks while re-recording his/her own contribution. Likewise, our lead guitarist can record one part, switch to another track, and record another. And if we later decide that the vocals should be louder, we just push up the appropriate track's fader when we're mixing down from the multi-track master to stereo.

We can take these ideas further. A solo muso can effectively play every part in a complex arrangement, simply by recording them one after another on separate tracks. Or, if the bassist decides two months later that

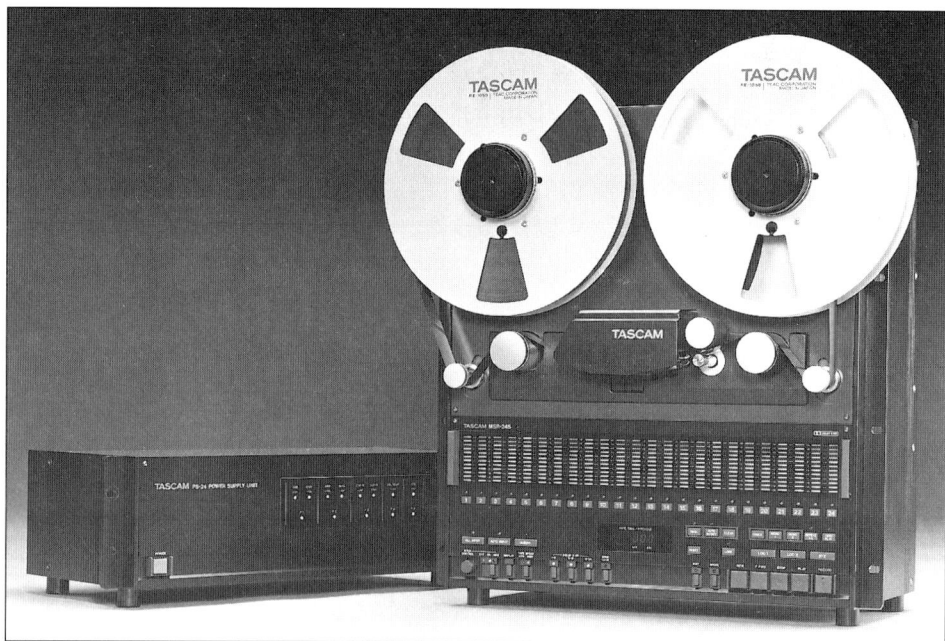

Even 24-track recording is now 'affordable' thanks to products like Tascam's MSR-24S

he's got a better bass line, just re-record that one track. And if you want different mixes for different purposes (like album and radio or club versions), you just mix the existing tracks differently.

So far, it seems that multi-track beats direct-to-stereo hollow, and for most purposes, that is indeed the case. But there's a little matter of money involved here – more tracks cost more money. So when we're talking about four- or even maybe eight-track, there may well not be enough tracks to give every musical element its own track. And, basically, there's no way out of this. The nearest thing to a solution is what goes under such names as...

TRACK BOUNCING, COLLAPSING, SUBMIXING OR PING-PONGING

What a mouthful. But the fact is that these are all different (and fairly non-explanatory) terms for the same trick. I'm going to call it track bouncing because, in the UK at least, that's the most commonly-used name.

Let's consider life with a four-track – you record maybe bass, drums and rhythm guitar, each on their own track. If all you want to add is lead vocal, no probs, because you've still got one track free. But if you've still got vocals, lead guitar and keyboards to record, then something has to be done. And what we do is to play back the three basic tracks, mix them together, and copy or 'bounce' the mix onto the unused fourth track. This frees up the original three tracks for new material. We could even add one of the new parts as we're doing this copying – if there's a mistake, the three basic tracks are still safe, so we just repeat the process. But...

Once we start to re-use the original tape tracks for recording new material, we lose what was recorded before, so we can't go back and remix that three-into-one track bounce. Make no mistake, the implications of this are pretty serious. Because what you have to do when bouncing is not only judge the balance between the musical elements you've already recorded, but also anticipate how that balance may be affected by everything you've still to record. Worse, there's a sound quality loss involved in the copying (at least there is with analogue).

But let's not get too depressed. Fact is, "Sgt Pepper" was recorded in pretty much this way – true, they had two four-tracks, but there was an awful lot of bouncing. Also, I've heard quite a few amateur four-track demos where I really couldn't criticise the overall mix balance. But track bouncing does fall short of the multi-track ideal of keeping every element separate, so that you leave all mix decisions until the final mixdown to stereo. This, of course, is why the big boys use 24, 32 or even 48 tracks.

MICROPHONES, EFFECTS & MONITORING

It would have been inconceivable 20 years ago, but today there are recording studios without even a single microphone – everything is created electronically. This is fine, but the majority of musos do need a mike at least sometimes, be it for vocals, guitar or drums. The really important question is how many mikes you need at the same time, which in turn depends both on what you're recording, and how you're recording it. There's a world of difference between recording a band one instrument at a time, and recording everything in a single take. According to an old professional saying, it's better to have one good mike than five cheap ones, but this is precious little comfort if you actually need five.

More than any other area of recording, effects have been dramatically changed by the development of affordable digital technology. This means that you can currently get a perfectly credible reverb for under £200, while even a multi-effect processor with several dozen different effects may cost less than £500. Just as with keyboard voices, there is a seemingly insatiable demand for 'new' effects, where 'new' usually means variations and combinations of existing effects.

While effects are definitely 'sexy', monitoring is equally definitely the Cinderella of most amateur and semi-pro recording. This is understandable in one sense, because monitoring gear doesn't directly contribute anything to the recording process. But indirectly... well, if you can't hear it, you can't fix it or mix it – which is, I guess, why so many musos produce demos that principally demonstrate either some astonishing ideas on mix balance and EQ (perfectly possible), or a complete inability to hear what they're doing. This is OK if you're just making tapes for your own amusement, but not really conducive to convincing somebody else of your competence (stand by for more of this diatribe in the *Monitoring* chapter).

MIDI, VIRTUAL TRACKS & SYNC

Most musicians, and probably all keyboardists, will know something about MIDI (Musical Instrument Digital Interface). When MIDI was new, around a decade ago, its first use was in enabling different makes of equipment to 'talk to' one another. This meant that a master keyboard could control several different synth modules. Then sequencers became popular, allowing MIDI 'event' and 'timing' information to be stored, so that a performance involving several MIDI instruments could be put together one instrument at a time, and all played back in unison.

The term 'virtual track' simply refers to the output from each sequenced instrument (where there are several outputs, as in many drum boxes, each output is called a virtual track). For some kinds of music, such as instrumental dance material, these virtual tracks may be all that's needed – simply feed them to a mixer, and record the result direct to stereo. But perhaps you also want vocals and/or guitar. Irrespective of whether you record these 'live' elements on cassette, open-reel or digital, you need some way of synchronising their playback with the MIDI virtual tracks. Ignoring the special cases where the recorder has a dedicated sync or 'timecode' track, most systems work by recording a sync signal on one of the audio tracks, enabling the recorder and sequencer(s) to play in time.

As we'll see in the MIDI chapter, there's usually rather more to syncing than this very general explanation, but the basic idea has two big attractions: first, you can have as many sequenced instruments as you like, all synced from just one tape track; second, because the synced and sequenced instruments are playing 'live' at mixdown time, you avoid the inevitable sound quality losses involved in recording them on tape.

FEATURES, SOUND QUALITY & RELIABILITY

None of these items come free, so unless you've got a limitless budget, you'll almost certainly have to accept a compromise in one or more areas. Features are usually the one aspect that buyers aren't prepared to compromise on, which is fair enough, because if you haven't got the features you actually need, you can't do the job the gear's intended for. The two most obvious considerations here are the number of mixer channels and recorder tracks.

*Acceptable compromise? Yamaha's MT-8X eight-tracker only records **four tracks at once***

As far as sound quality is concerned, I would divide equipment performance into three rough 'n' ready categories: notepad, demo, and release. To define these a little, notepad performance is basically for your own ears only – it simply gives you a record of your musical ideas. Demo quality is for other people to listen to, but the actual sound quality is of secondary importance to the musical content. Release quality means that it's good enough to ask people to pay money for.

Trouble is, there's an awful lot of overlap here. For example, it might be tempting to assume that cassette recording means notepad and demo, while open-reel means release. But Michelle Shocked's "Campfire Tapes" album was recorded on a portable cassette recorder, and PJ Harvey's four-track demos have been commercially released. At the other extreme, picking an example without prejudice, Brian May's "Driven By You" CD single was recorded in a top-line pro studio, but the final sound quality is well below that possible with a high-speed multi-track cassette machine.

Reliability is actually a catch-all term for several items: reliability itself (how long between breakdowns), total life expectancy, and service back-up. Clearly, there is a big difference between the workload in a home studio and a pro studio, but, sooner or later, mixer controls do become noisy, and tape heads do wear out. Not surprisingly, if you want longer, more reliable life, and better back-up when things do go wrong, then you're going to pay a higher price to start with. This is important, because we're not talking about a small increase in price – a true pro item can easily cost three times as much as its semi-pro equivalent.

PRICES & DISCOUNTS

I could save this for the *System Planning & Budgeting* chapter, but between here and there I'm going to be mentioning, and assessing, quite a number of products. It's only natural that assessment involves taking price into account, but the problem is: what price?

On the one hand, there's what's commonly called the 'suggested retail price' – this sometimes means what you can actually expect to pay, but more often means what a retailer would like you to pay, but doesn't really expect you to. Discounts can vary dramatically and frequently, which means that 'real' value for money can only be judged at the time you're buying. This makes it difficult for me to judge, and since there really isn't a satisfactory way out, I'm going to take the easiest, and work with 'suggested' prices. I mention this now so you're not surprised when you find me talking about price-tags that bear little resemblence to 'real' prices.

TECH-TALK

J ust as it is with cars, there's an awful lot of stuff you could know, but only a little that's necessary to get by. Here it is...

FREQUENCY
Musicians call it pitch, and describe it as such-and-such a note; for frequency we measure it in Hertz and kiloHertz (1kHz = 1000Hz). Small Hertz numbers are the same as low-pitched bass notes, while large numbers, as in kHz, are the same as very high-pitched treble ones. Doubling or halving a frequency is the same as shifting the corresponding note up or down an octave. A tone made up of just a single frequency is actually both very boring and very annoying, and 'real' musical notes are made up of many different frequencies, the lowest of which is called the fundamental, and the higher-frequency components of which are known as harmonics. Among other things, it is variations in the make-up of these harmonics that give each instrument its own distinctive sound.

Bottom E on a standard bass guitar is 42Hz, the human voice and its harmonics principally cover around 50Hz–8kHz, and cymbals are still producing harmonics above 20kHz. Most pro-quality audio gear is expected to handle frequencies from 20Hz–20kHz, and even though music can include audible information both below and above these frequencies, this ten-octave range is the generally accepted standard.

DECIBELS
Commonly abbreviated to dB, a deciBel is not actually a measure of anything – it simply expresses the difference between two numbers. Sometimes this is useful, but many times it isn't, because though it's nice to know that one bag

of sugar weighs twice as much as another, it's a jolly sight better to know how much the first one actually weighs. What we need here is a 'reference', where we simply say that 0dB equals a certain amount of whatever it is we're measuring. Fine. Problem is that there are many such references, and we end up with lots of different standards, such as dBV, dBm, dBu, dBA and a whole load more.

Fortunately, there's seldom any need to get involved in what these mean and the differences between them. Suffice to say that when it comes to signal levels, we have items like mikes and guitars, with outputs that may be anything from -60dB to 0dB, and 'line-level' sources like keyboards, drum boxes, and effects, where there are two standards: -10dB and +4dB. The former may be considered 'amateur', because it was created to enable early home recording gear to connect with domestic hi-fi; the +4dB standard is true pro. The existence of these two 'standard' levels can lead to problems: running a -10dB source into a +4dB input means noise and hiss will be 14dB louder than it could be; running +4dB into -10dB risks overload distortion. By and large, you won't have to worry overmuch in practice – most modern gear (except some super-pro items, identifiable by super-pro prices) either runs at -10dB or caters for both standards.

Apart from describing input and output levels, dBs are most often encountered in the form of record levels. It's worth noting that there's a considerable difference between analogue and digital here – while analogue record levels can happily go above 0dB (usually to at least +4dB on cassette four-tracks, maybe as high as +10dB on open-reels), digital signals must never exceed 0dB, or there's immediate and nasty overload distortion.

SOUND LEVELS

Often referred to as SPL (sound pressure level), and usually measured in a version of the dB called a dBA. The dear old '0dB reference' in this case is a very, very quiet sound, and background noise in the 'average' living-room comes in at around 30dBA. Normal conversation runs 65–70dBA, a noisy city street is around 90dBA, a 'typical' pub band delivers maybe 110dBA at close quarters, and a Jumbo Jet taking off can hit 135. Long-term (as in months rather than minutes) exposure to anything over 100dBA brings a real risk of permanent hearing damage (I know: real rockers and ravers don't wear earplugs, but then others don't tell you the time when you ask the way to the Gents...).

DYNAMIC RANGE

In principle at least, this is simply the difference between low-level unwanted background noise, and the highest signal level that can be produced. And because dynamic range is a measure of difference, it's measured in simple dBs. The dynamic range of music can be tremendous: a band could easily produce 120dBA peaks in a venue where the ambient 'noise-floor' is 30dBA – this gives us a dynamic range of 90dB. Interestingly, this is just about the same dynamic range that pro studios aim for, while a four-track may struggle to give much above 60dB.

UNBALANCED AND BALANCED

Respectively amateur and professional, an unbalanced connection uses two wires, while a balanced one has three – two for the signal plus a third outer wire that acts as a 'screen', protecting the signal-carrying wires from hum and other interference pick-up. Balanced is clearly superior, but also more

Most mikes have balanced outputs, but most budget multi-track inputs are unbalanced

expensive. The resulting situation is quite a mess – most microphones have balanced outputs, but most cassette multi-track inputs are unbalanced; separate mixers generally have balanced mike inputs, but the line ins could be balanced or unbalanced. Fortunately, nothing dire happens if you mix balanced and unbalanced – all that occurs is that you lose the benefits of balanced operation.

IMPEDANCE

We could devote quite a bit of mental energy to this one, but there's really no need – with only a very few exceptions, you can connect just about any signal source to any input, without bothering about low or high impedance and 'Ohms' stuff – if the levels (as in dBs) match, the impedances will too.

The first exceptional case is actually quite common: electric guitar. What counts here is that, though you can feed guitar straight into a mike or mike/line input, you could well get a better sound by using a DI box. The other cases that need mentioning are high- and dual-impedance microphones. High-impedance mikes are usually very cheap and equally nasty, but dual (high/low) mikes are quite common in the £30–70 range – this is fine, provided you can select the low-impedance setting by switch (preferably a locking type), but not good when it involves rewiring connector pins.

TECH-SPECS

This is the small-print you find at the back of sales leaflets and instruction manuals. Some of it can be useful, such as whether line connections are -10dB or +4dB, and the range of EQ controls. But many tech-specs are not only irrelevant, they're potentially downright misleading. There are two fundamental problems here: the use of different 'standards' for supposedly identical measurements, and the fact that many measurements don't directly relate to audible performance in the real world. We could devote many pages to explaining the whys and wherefores of this; suffice to say that any piece of equipment has many aspects to its performance, and though we can debate about what to measure, and how to measure it, there is simply no known way of putting all these measurements together to form a single 'sound quality' rating.

Ultimately, you can only rely on critical listening, and reputation/recommendation. Given this situation, there doesn't seem to be much point exploring tech-specs in detail, and we'll be better employed looking at what the various items of equipment do, and then how to get them to do it...

PART ONE
HARDWARE

MIXER FEATURES

Something to aspire to? How things look from the driving seat of an SSL desk

At its simplest, a mixer is just two or more inputs, each with its own volume control, and an output which carries the combined signals. And, at the other extreme, you could have a hundred-channel console with around ten thousand individual controls, and a half-million-pound price tag.

The most immediately obvious features of a mixer are the number of input channels, the facilities on each channel, and the number of output channels (known as groups). Every mixer has its own (pardon the pun) mix of features, so the variations are almost endless. You'll find some thoughts on the practical aspects of choosing a mixer 'package' that suits your needs at the end of this chapter, but first we'll take a moderately-detailed look at the features themselves, starting with…

MAIN INPUT CHANNELS

MIKE, LINE, AND MIKE/LINE INPUTS

On the face of it, these might seem straightforward enough, but there are actually several variations. The cheapest and simplest, as found on most cassette multi-tracks, is a combined mike and line input. This will be an unbalanced jack, and the difference in levels between mike and line sources is catered for by a gain/trim control (see below).

Most outboard mixers have separate mike and line inputs for each main channel – the mike will almost always be a balanced XLR, and the line an unbalanced or balanced jack, depending on price. On all but the cheapest desks, you can expect to find phantom power on the mike inputs – this means that the XLR can supply the juice (48V) to run a condenser mike. If there's even the slightest chance you'll ever be able to afford a condenser (or hire one), this is a 'must-have' feature, as you'll otherwise have to spend an almost unbelievable £100-plus on a dedicated power supply. Phantom power is usually switchable, either channel-by-channel or with one all-channel switch.

It's important to know that there are potential problems here: you can use a balanced dynamic/electret mike into a phantom-power-on input, but *not* an unbalanced source, such as a guitar, keyboard or drum box. Connecting such a source will very possibly 'shut-down' phantom-powering to all channels; alternatively it could blow a hard-to-replace internal fuse, and it might even damage the output circuit of the signal source. These problems are entirely avoided by always terminating unbalanced leads with a jack (never an XLR), so you'll always feed unbalanced sources into the dedicated line input jacks.

On some desks, physically plugging-in to the line jack will automatically disconnect the mike input; on others there's the convenience (and expense) of a selector switch.

GAIN/TRIM AND PAD

These controls adjust the input to handle the vastly different signal levels a channel may have to cope with – anything from a low-output mike on a quiet instrument (maybe -50dB), through to a condenser on a bass drum or trumpet (over 0dB). Where the input is a combined mike/line, it may also be faced with line levels as high as +16dB on peaks. On desks that have separate mike and line inputs, gain may work only on the mike signal. Gain controls are generally calibrated in dBs, but in practical use they're just like a volume control: you turn them up for more gain, and down for less. A gain control is set right when you get a mixer/recorder meter reading of around 0dB for a main fader setting of 0dB (7–8 on many cassette multi-tracks). A pad switch simply reduces signal levels by a fixed amount, usually 10 or 20dB.

EQ (EQUALISATION)

Equalisation is just a fancy name for tone controls. But though some EQ can be as simple as hi-fi-type bass 'n' treble, there are many more powerful versions. Even b 'n' t comes in several varieties: the two basic kinds are known as 'peaking' and 'shelving'. These are most easily explained by the example of a bass control set to full boost...

Starting in the midrange (1000Hz) and working our way down to the bass end, we find that both EQ types introduce increasing boost as the frequency is reduced (maybe +2dB at 700Hz, and +5dB at 250Hz). By the time we reach the midbass (say 80–100Hz), both provide a similar amount of boost (maybe +10dB), but from here on down, the two types behave very differently. On a peaking bass, the boost starts to decrease below its peak frequency (also called its 'turnover point'), so that by 40Hz the boost may be down to +3dB, and by 20Hz there's no boost at all. By contrast, a shelving control reaches its maximum boost around, say, 80Hz, and this level of boost is then maintained all the way down to below 20Hz. Both designs have their (different) uses, but most modern mixers opt for shelving types.

There's also the little matter of the 'turnover' or peak frequencies. Traditionally, these were usually 80–100Hz and 10kHz, but current design (and many users) favour 60Hz and 12kHz.

The first step up from b 'n' t is to add a midrange boost/cut control. It is often said that a simple mid control like this is fairly useless, the argument being that, for example, cutting the mid has exactly the same effect as boosting the bass and treble. This is often true, as far as it goes, but it doesn't go far enough. Cutting or boosting all three ranges at the same time produces frequency response/tonal effects that can't be achieved with just bass and treble.

Still, the bottom/mid/top formula *is* fairly limited – fortunately it's also much less common than the souped-up version: bass, treble and sweep mid. Sweep adds a second control to the basic boost/cut knob for the frequency range in question. In the case of a sweep mid, the sweep control varies the 'centre' boost/cut frequency from maybe 250Hz (low-mid) through to 5kHz (mid-treble). In practical musical terms, this makes it far more useful than fixed-frequency mid EQ, enabling you, for example, to 'tune in' to guitar fundamentals or harmonics, snare drum shell resonance, and vocal 'depth' or 'presence'.

Sweep EQ is often called parametric, but this is really something of a con-job – true parametric EQ adds a third control to the pair used for sweep; the newcomer rather mysteriously being called Q. Q is actually an electronics term, probably best illustrated by the way some Q controls are labelled 'wide' at one end and 'narrow' at the other. A wide setting means that the boost/cut control affects a broad range of frequencies either side of the centre frequency set by the sweep knob. A narrow setting means that only frequencies close to the centre are boosted or cut. Parametric is highly desirable, since it enables you to customise EQ to your exact requirements; trouble is, it only features on fairly upmarket mixers – you can however buy outboard parametric EQ as an effect processor.

The final type of EQ we'll consider here is the simplest: what's called a lo-cut/hi-pass filter. This 'rolls-off' or cuts low bass – you'd maybe use it on vocals, although its main application is in live recording and PA, where it can reduce ambient noise such as traffic and air-conditioning, floor-borne noise like footfalls, or PA bass-bin boom.

Some mixers, such as many line/submixer jobs, don't have any EQ at all, while basic cassette multi-tracks may only have EQ on the stereo busses (see later), not the individual channels. As the price increases, so does the flexibility – an upper-midmarket desk might feature bass, two sweep mids, treble, and a lo-cut bass filter, plus an EQ in/out switch to enable quick with/without comparisons. (Knowledgeable types will notice I haven't mentioned graphic EQ – that's because I don't know of a single mixer where it appears on the input channels, so we'll save it for *Effects*.)

CHANNEL INSERTS

These can be extremely useful and, with a technically well-designed mixer, they cost very little to provide, which makes their absence from many cassette multi-tracks and from quite a few mixers seriously annoying. An insert uses a stereo/three-pole jack, combining both unbalanced line output (send) and unbalanced line input (return) on a single socket. This is handy for patching an effect (such as a compressor) into just a single channel.

AUX/EFFECT AND CUE/FOLDBACK SENDS

Four names, two main jobs, and anything from one to a dozen knobs. The basic idea is simple though: whether you're feeding an effect processor such as reverb, or setting up foldback, you may want the mix of channel signals to be different from that at the main outputs. A couple of examples: you want the bass guitar fairly loud in your mix, but you don't want it to receive much reverb, so you keep the effect send control on that channel set low; at the same time, you're providing a cue/foldback mix to the drummer, and he/she wants the bass guitar much louder than it is in the main mix, so you set the appropriate send up high.

Basic cassette multi-tracks generally have two sends: one labelled 'aux' (auxilliary) or 'effect', and primarily intended for use with reverb, the second often separate from the main channels, and enabling you to create a 'cue'/monitor mix of already-recorded tracks for foldback. Between them, these two sends will fully satisfy many users' needs, but that's a long way from saying that they'll satisfy everyone. For example, you might want a second effect send for an exciter or flanger, and a band might want different foldback mixes for each member, especially if the desk is doing double-duty in PA.

Sends come in two 'flavours': pre- and post-fader. Post-fader is the more common on budget mixers, and usually the more useful – the send signal is taken after EQ and fader, so changes in these affect the send. This is the way you'll generally want things when, for example, feeding a reverb. But you might want the alternative pre-fader (and usually pre-EQ) send so that a foldback mix doesn't get altered when you play with the main channel faders. On some desks, one or more sends may be switchable pre/post. Also, you'll find mixers and cassette multi-tracks that combine two sends on one control knob – this cuts costs slightly, but means you can't drive both sends at once, potentially limiting usefulness. There should also be a master level control for each send.

GROUP ASSIGNS AND PAN
On a two-group/stereo desk you'll find only a pan control, which acts just like the balance control on a stereo amp: you can move or 'pan' the mono channel signal anywhere across the stereo soundstage, from hard left, through centre, over to hard right. Groups (see below) generally have their assigns (fancy name for select buttons) combined into odd and even-numbered pairs (1-2, 3-4, etc), so you select a pair group (say, 7-8), then pan between them, 7-left, 8-right, and 12 o'clock (centre of the stereo soundstage) to feed both groups .

OVERLOAD/CLIP LEDs
Overload distortion is audibly nasty, and a channel LED can help locate the source of such trouble quickly. Some such indicators only show overload at the input end of the channel, which, though often helpful, means that they don't light when distortion occurs further on in the signal's progress through the channel (for example, too high a return from an insert effect, or two sweep EQs set to full boost at the same frequency). Some mid-market desks do provide LEDs that monitor this sort of naughtiness, and they're generally recognisable by the fact that the LED will be close to the EQ section. The (expensive) ideal is to have LEDs on both the gain/trim and post-EQ stages.

MAIN FADER
Main volume control might be a better name because, though most volume controls are linear sliders, many line/submixers, and even a few 'main' mixers, use rotaries. In some applications, rotaries are good, because they take up less space, are less likely to get knocked off their settings, and are generally both

cheaper and more reliable. But for hands-on production mixing most people strongly prefer sliders, partly because it's easier to assess channel levels at a glance, but also because they make ducking, fading and gain-riding (see *Mixing*) far easier to control.

MUTE

Simply an on/off switch for the channel output. This can be extremely handy when mixing down a multi-track tape. There may well be several tracks that have nothing useful on them for much of the time (say, a keyboard or guitar that only comes in on choruses); rather than leave the channel 'open' during 'dead air', which lets tape hiss and any unwanted mike pick-up into the mix, it is better to 'close' or 'kill' the channel when it isn't actually wanted.

DIRECT OUTPUTS

These carry each channel's signal as it leaves the channel and heads for the groups. In many situations, they probably won't be used at all, but two potentially important applications are triggering effects/samples, and feeding direct to a tape track. The current trend on mid-market desks is to allow the output signal to be switched between direct channel and group, which can greatly reduce the need for repatching.

BUSSES AND OUTPUT GROUPS

A buss is simply a signal path that can have different inputs and outputs connected to it – we've actually met them already in the form of aux/effect and cue/foldback sends. An output group is just a particular type of buss: one which gets its input signal from the outputs of the channels, taken after the main fader, group assigns and pan. At the least, a group will have its own fader (also called a master), except on some stereo/two-group mixers, where the two faders use a single control knob, making it easier to maintain stereo balance. There may also be a group insert (like a channel insert), and/or a direct input to each group, usually called buss in – these are useful for connecting an extra (sub)mixer, or indeed any line-level signal source that has its own volume control.

AUX/EFFECT RETURNS

These inputs to the group buss(es) enable you to bring the output(s) of effect processor(s) back into the mix. With the exception of mono/one-group mixers, you'll almost always find a minimum of two mono or one stereo return, pretty much essential when you consider that the most common effect is reverb, and almost all modern digital reverbs have stereo outputs. Aux/effect returns differ from ordinary buss inputs, in that they have level

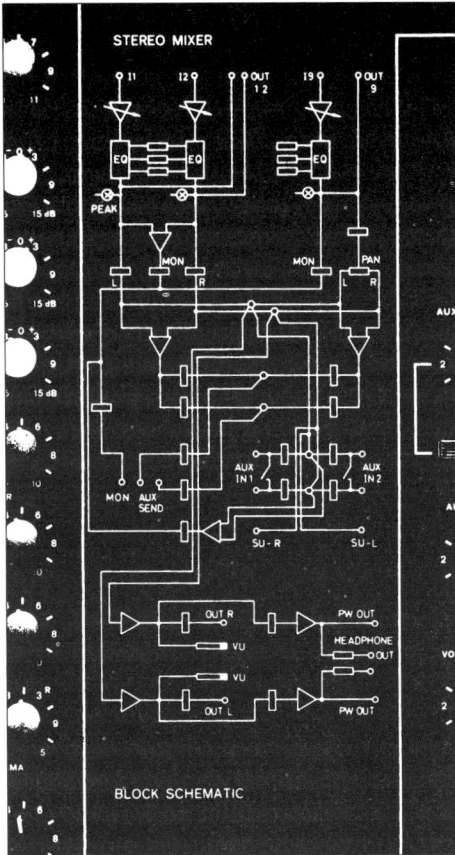

Left: simple mixer block diagram; right: output groups (with black faders) on Spirit desk

controls (plus group assigns and pan on desks with more than two groups). As the price rises, you might find EQ (probably simple two-band) on the returns.

MONITORS

On basic cassette multi-tracks, the monitor section may be as simple as just a level control for each tape track, mixed together with whatever is on the stereo buss, and feeding a phones socket plus, hopefully, phono sockets to drive a power amp and speakers. In this situation, monitoring and foldback are pretty much one and the same thing. But once we get to upmarket cassette multi-tracks and separate mixers, monitoring becomes a much more flexible and powerful tool. A full-blown monitor section allows you to select just about anything that's going on in the mixer, and feed it to your speakers or phones, without disturbing the main mix(es) in the slightest. You can expect selector buttons for each of the main groups, and hopefully for each effect/ foldback send, possibly plus each of the effect returns. There may be facilities for listening to one or more stereo recorders, and on some desks these can be selected to work as extra stereo buss inputs.

SOLO/PFL/AFL/SOLO-IN-PLACE

Solo buttons may be found on the individual input channels, the output groups and even on the effect returns – pressing one temporarily mutes whatever the monitor section is set to, replacing it with just the signal on that one channel or group. This can be very useful indeed, enabling quick assessment of EQ or inserted effects, and tracing the source of distortion/weird noises. PFL (pre-fade listen) and AFL (after-fade listen) both have their uses; a refinement is 'solo-in-place', perhaps better-described as 'solo-in-stereo', because the channel signal is taken after the pan control, so you can hear its location on the stereo soundstage. Many solos only work for as long as the button is held down, which can be a real nuisance if you want to waggle noisy cables or tweak an inserted effect while soloing – so look for 'locking' or 'latching' buttons. A solo master level control is a useful extra.

IN-LINE MONITORS

At their simplest, these start out as the tape track level controls needed on even the simplest cassette multi-track, but re-located so that each track's control knob is on the similarly-numbered main-channel 'strip'. The really important addition is a switch on each channel, commonly labelled 'main/tape' or 'channel/monitor'. In the 'main' position, the mike or line input uses all the channel's major facilities, like EQ, aux sends and fader, and the tape track input has just the monitor controls. In the 'tape' position, the tape signal gets to use the channel-proper, and the mike/line signal goes through what were the monitor controls.

Let's consider what this means in practice. You use the 'main' position for laying down live tracks, because the simple monitor controls will be sufficient to give you a cue/foldback mix of the tracks you've already recorded. And then, come mixdown time, you switch to 'tape', so you can sweeten the raw track signals with EQ and effects. Simple. But there's more…

Many musicians are combining 'real' tape tracks with 'virtual' sequenced tracks. Naturally, you need enough channels to handle the total number of tracks, whatever their origin. But many channels cost mucho mazuma, and you may well find you're prepared to compromise, for example by accepting that your virtual tracks get less sweetening than real tracks – in which case, you can use the in-line monitor controls to bring in your virtual tracks at mixdown time. Thing is, though, you may equally well find that your virtual tracks do need some sweetening, and this is why an increasing number of mid- and up-market mixers provide far more flexibility than a simple 'main/tape' selector. Examples include what's often called a 'flip' switch, assigning the EQ to main or tape inputs, while more expensive desks allow you to 'split' the channel EQ, so some parts work on the main input, and others on the monitor. Effect/foldback sends may be selectable to work on either input, and it's also handy if the monitor has its own solo.

Even with all these features, in-line desks inevitably fall short of the ideal of having a full complement of facilities for every input, not least because you have to choose which of two signals gets the fader, the other usually being consigned to a tiny rotary knob – bad news if you want to duck, fade, gain-ride or otherwise tweak both levels during a mix. Fortunately, many users find that their virtual tracks don't need much 'hands-on' work during mixdown, so in-line monitoring, with its effective doubling of the number of channels for less than double the cost, works well – so much so that it's now pretty much the norm on recording mixers costing, say, £1000 and up.

METERS

Signal levels, whether within a mixer or going onto tape, are always important – too low, too much noise; too high, too much distortion. But there's metering, and there's metering...

Soundtracs Solo desks with (above) moving needle, (below) LED metering

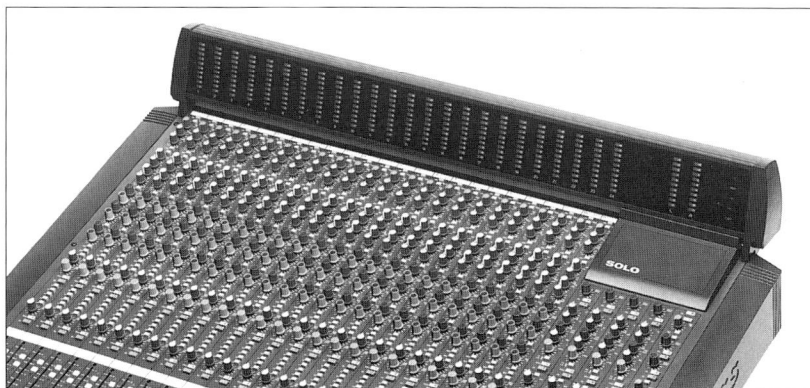

MOVING-NEEDLE METERS

With the rare (and expensive) exception of what are called PPMs (peak programme meters), moving-needle meters (sometimes known as VUs) suffer from a fundamental problem: the needles move too slowly to show the short-term signal peaks that can overload electronics, analogue tape, and just about anything digital. They're still useful for displaying average levels (for example, to make sure different songs have the same overall level when putting together a compilation). but for most purposes they've largely been replaced by...

LED/LCD/FLUORESCENT METERS

By far the most common type on everything from cassette multi-tracks, through FX, and on to top-line consoles. They have two potential advantages over ordinary moving-needle meters: they're usually more legible, especially when multi-coloured, and they can be much faster-responding. Keyword, though, is *can*... There are many such meters, on both multi-track cassette recorders and mixers, that don't respond remotely as fast as they might, so they still don't reveal the signal peaks they're there for.

Metering is really all about visual level monitoring, and just like the audio monitor side, there is a strong case for flexibility – big pro consoles have a full complement of channel, group and effect meters, and these facilities are available as a 'meter-bridge' option on some upper-mid-market desks. One look at the prices of such metering explains why most designers keep the meter-count down, typically to one per group. As with audio monitoring, it is possible to increase the flexibility here, for example by switching the meters from groups to effect sends and/or returns, the stereo mix, and, ideally, solo. This last is particularly useful, since it effectively allows you to meter individual channels.

AUTOMATION

This is just a clever name for mixer sequencing, which in turn is only a variation on keyboard sequencing – the mixer (or its associated computer) stores a list of what you want it to do, and when you want it to do it.

At its simplest, this will be just the ability to mute (and un-mute) channels automatically, useful for killing 'dead air' noise when a source/tape track isn't contributing anything. Next up, sometimes, is the ability to change group assigns for each channel, and possibly also the effect return assigns. There are some real creative possibilities here – hence the success of Tascam's MIDIstudios – but there are also many music types and recording approaches that simply don't need these facilities (as distinct from basic 'mute'). And then comes the bit almost everybody's interested in: fader automation. The idea here is that you can practise your ducking, gain-riding etc, until you're happy, and then the desk will do it all automatically come final mixdown. Nice idea...

Spirit Auto desk with VCA fader automation provided by outboard computer

There are two main types of fader automation, called VCA and moving-fader. VCA stands for voltage-controlled amplifier, and what it means is that, like most sequenced things, the up-down fading happens electronically (that is, invisibly, so the 'hands-on' fader control doesn't move). The fader 'setting' may go up and down, but the actual physical fader, he don't move a millimetre. Some, possibly many, users have no problem with this, and are quite happy setting up the level changes they want via an on-board, QWERTY or musical keyboard. Others aren't. Which happens to be tough luck, because true moving-fader automation is still the financial preserve of big pro studios and people who employ accountants...

Most mute, assign and VCA control is based on MIDI. Basic mute and possibly assign facilities may well be controlled by an on-board microcomputer, hopefully with both battery memory backup and some means of dumping/archiving the data (as in the MIDIstudios' ability to save and load using the actual multitrack cassette). Some VCA desks also use on-board computers, but others require the programs and data to live in an out-board computer such as a PC, Mac or Atari. This approach makes sense if you're also going to use the computer for sequencing virtual tracks, though the actual VCA software could still sting you for £300 (ludicrous, given what a simple program it is). If you've no other use for a computer, you might well want to compare prices of all-in-one desks against desk+computer+software.

Beyond even moving-fader automation lies the concept of 'total recall' (which has nothing to do with Arnold Schwarzenegger). Basic total recall simply senses and remembers control settings, then displays them on a monitor – the user has to actually move the EQ, effects and other knobs until they match. This is way short of the ideal of fully automated and sequenced mixing. If *that's* what you want, you'll most likely be interested in...

26

DIGITAL MIXING

As of right now (Summer '94), digital mixers probably account for less than one percent of the market. The problem is largely down to price – partly for the necessary analogue-to-digital and digital-to-analogue converters, but more for the sheer processing power and speed needed to do digital EQ (and other effects) on several channels at once, and at the same time produce several different mixes (as in, groups and sends to outboard effects). Still, hardware prices continue to fall, and there seems little doubt that digital is the way the industry is going – in the long term. Meanwhile, many digital mixing products are associated with hard-disk recording (see *Multi-track Recorder Types*), which certainly has its advantages of near-instant access and non-destructive editing, though at a higher price than tape-based systems.

Yamaha DMP-7: pioneer of 'affordable' digital mixing, forerunner of ProMix

PUTTING IT ALL TOGETHER

While the number of mixer channels you need (whether main or main plus in-line monitors), and their facilities, are usually fairly straightforward, life can get more difficult when it comes to the number of groups. This is important, because extra groups make for a pretty dramatic price rise.

Once upon a time, the idea was to have as many groups as tape tracks. This makes sense when, for example, you're recording a whole band in a single take, or when you want to be able to route any input channel to any tape track. But many people don't work that way – depending on how you're handling drums, you might well be recording only one or two tracks at a time. In this case, a stereo/two-group desk could actually work quite adequately, even running 16/24 tracks, though of course you have to patch outputs to the tracks you're recording – arguably a small price, given the cost-saving relative to extra groups.

Though this multi-track-to-stereo desk idea may be one extreme, the alter-end of a group per track is actually quite rare these days. Some eight-track users get along quite happily with four-group mixers, while many 16/24 buyers seem happy with eight groups. I don't think anyone is claiming it's ideal, but it certainly seems to offer an acceptable cost/flexibility balance for most of the people, most of the time.

What leads on from this is the classic 'channels-to-groups' summary of a mixer, for example, 16:2 – 16 channel inputs to stereo/two-group output. This gets complicated when you consider desks with in-line monitoring, which for example may give a 16-channel mixer 32 inputs (assuming there's a monitor on every channel, which ain't always so). Also complicating matters, there is, for example, a considerable difference between a 16:8 and a 16:8:2. On the former, groups 1 and 2 or 7 and 8 are used for the final stereo mix (look for the ability to assign the outputs of other groups to those used for stereo – this enables you to use these other groups for 'submixes' such as stereo drums). A 16:8:2 uses all eight groups to feed a separate stereo mix, which is slightly more useful, more expensive, and more common.

Cassette multi-tracks (and some mixers) manage to confuse matters even more, for example by having some mike/line and some line-only inputs. The mixer side of cassette machines is generally stereo/two-group, but with the ability to send the first four inputs direct to the same-numbered tracks.

You may well find that getting what you want in one mixer department involves having, and paying for, more than you need in another – for example, if you want really flexible EQ, you'll quite possibly end up with many more effect/foldback sends than you'll use.

Beyond the simple but essential feature-count, there's a whole world involving the 'feel' of a mixer. To give some examples: do you want your connectors on-top or round the back? Do the control knobs have different-coloured end-caps and clear position indicators? Can you easily see whether buttons are up or down? Do the faders have enough travel and do they feel both light and smooth? Is there space to write an input/track ident above or below each channel fader? These sorts of things can make or break the practicalities and pleasures of engineering and production.

MIXER MODELS

So many mixers, so little space, so... rather than pick an assortment to represent the vast variety on offer, but which wouldn't allow room to compare competitors, I've zeroed-in on just one type: eight-group mixers (with one exception, but as you'll see when we come to it, it's a pretty important exception). I chose eight rather than four-group types, because the great majority of the latter are not in-line designs (see *Mixer Features*).

Allen & Heath GS3: comes with 16, 24 (as above) or 32 inputs

ALLEN & HEATH GS3 – £2583

This price gives you the 16:8:2 version – add £1240 for 24 inputs, plus £1275 to go to 32. Phantom, insert and direct out with channel/group switching to save re-patching. Three-band EQ with lo and mid sweeps and EQ in/out, four post-fader sends (splittable between channel and in-line), plus one pre-fader. The in-line monitor has its own two-band EQ and pre-fader send, along with a 'flip' switch. PFL solos and mutes on channels, in-lines, sends and groups. Four stereo returns with two-band EQ, solo and mute. Separate phones and main monitor selectors, plus two stereo tape connectors with copy switching. Full automation of all mutes, either using the onboard 32 'snapshot' memories, or from external MIDI control, plus seven programmable MIDI keys that could, for example, operate a MIDI-equipped multi-track.

FOSTEX 812 – £1100

Only 12 main inputs, but eight groups at the kind of price you'd often pay for four. Main inputs have phantom power, three-band EQ (lo and mid sweeps), and two sends. You can switch the in-line monitors to use the main channel facilities, but you actually have to replug to also use the monitor inputs for 'live' sources – potentially very annoying. Still, if you don't need the extra inputs, the in-lines can be switched to provide an extra (stereo) effect send. Locking AFL solo-in-place, and channel mutes that can use external MIDI control with the addition of the 8200 interface (£149). Three stereo returns and excellent meters with switchable peak-hold. Overall, you're effectively paying for the eight groups by accepting relatively limited channel facilities. Equally, if you want eight groups on a budget, the 812 is unbeatable on price.

MACKIE 8-BUSS – £2875

This price is for the 16:8:2; extra channels come in eight-input blocks at around £700. Main inputs have phantom, four-band EQ (sweep lo-mid, parametric hi-mid) with lo-cut filter and EQ in/out, up to six sends with pre/post switching, solo-in-place, signal and overload LEDs, inserts and direct outs, and in-line monitors with 'flip', EQ 'split' and send selection. Six stereo returns plus two stereo ins (these only go to the monitors), inserts and solos on the eight groups, two completely separate phones mixes as well as main monitor outputs. Group meters also show solo channel levels, and full channel metering is available as a bridge option (£649 for 16 channels, £799 for 32). VCA fader automation available 'soon', but will need an outboard computer.

SOUNDCRAFT SPIRIT STUDIO LC – £2230

This price is for the 16:8:2 version – another £700 buys the 24-in, and a

Soundcraft Spirit Studio: £2930 for the 24-input version

30

further £1000 gets you 32. Main inputs have phantom, insert, direct out (with a channel/group switch to save re-patching), three-band EQ with lo and mid sweeps, lo-cut filter and EQ in/out, plus an almost unbelievably flexible (and complicated) total of eight sends. In-line monitoring with 'flip' and send options, but no EQ 'split' – if you're not using the in-lines, you can add a further two sends, though Gawd knows what you'd need them all for. Overload LED, mute and switchable PFL solo/AFL solo-in-place. Three basic stereo returns, plus four more with short-throw faders, solos, mutes and group assigns. Group meters, PFL solos and inserts. Stereo tape ins can be routed to main mix, and very flexible monitoring options.

SOUNDTRACS TOPAZ – £3283
The price may seem high, but that's because you're getting 24 inputs – there's no 16 channel version, while going up to 32 adds £946. Channels have phantom, inserts, direct out with group switching to avoid re-patching, four-band EQ (lo and hi-mid sweeps) with EQ in/out, in-lines have their own two-band EQ plus 'flip'. Six sends (two pre), four of which are selectable for channel or monitor, four stereo returns. Solos and mutes on channels, in-lines, returns and groups. VCA automation, which will need an outboard computer, is 'under development'.

STUDIOMASTER P7 – £2580
This price is for the basic 16:8:2 version; further channels can be added in blocks of eight for just over £700 a unit. Main inputs offer line, mike and phantom, plus in-line monitors. Four-band EQ with two mid sweeps, six sends, main/monitor 'flip' plus an EQ 'split' facility. PFL and AFL solos, four stereo returns with two-band EQ, and connections for two stereo tape decks with copying. Automated mute on all channels, groups and four of the aux sends (but not returns). The automation provides 99 'snapshots', and can run on its own or under external MIDI control.

TASCAM M-2600 – £2499
This is the price for 16 channels – add £800 for 24. Channels provide phantom, inserts, direct/group outputs, four-band EQ (lo and hi-mid sweeps) with 'split' and 'flip', eight sends (six switchable pre/post, four configured as two stereo pairs). Six stereo returns, solos on channels, groups and returns, and mutes on all but the returns.

YAMAHA PROMIX 01 – £1879
Utterly and undeniably *the* sexy product of '94, the ProMix 01 is not only the cheapest digital mixer ever, but also throws in two effect processors, three stereo dynamics processors, and even motorised faders. There are 16 mike/line inputs (eight with XLRs and phantom power), plus a stereo line pair. All channels have digital three-band fully-parametric EQ, and four sends (two direct to the onboard effect processors). The effect returns and the main

stereo outputs also have three-band para. Every single mixer and effect setting is automated, and the built-in computer can store 50 'snapshots' of these settings, or you can use an external MIDI sequencer to store and execute as many snapshots as you like.

So far, the only word that springs to mind is 'awesome'. But... the ProMix is only stereo/two-group, and there are no channel outs, so it's no use in applications where you want to record more than two tracks at once – such as when recording a whole band live. Also, it isn't an in-line desk, and you actually have to repatch to change from live to tape inputs (strange, given how little the extra sockets and switching would have cost). Finally, and most

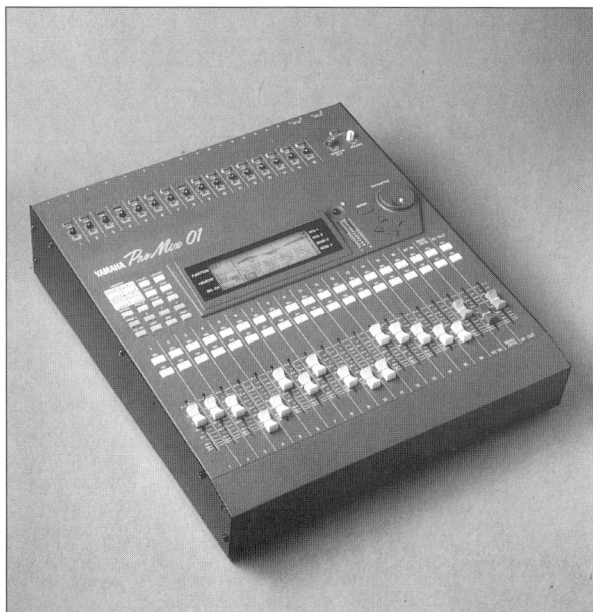

Yamaha ProMix: heralds affordable motorised faders

disappointingly, the inputs are analogue only, so you can't run digital sources such as an ADAT straight in – you have to go through the D/A and A/D process. But, as Yamaha point out, this is one reason why the desk is so cheap.

Every recording magazine is going ga-ga over ProMix, so this is a good place to point out that, sexy though it is, you do need to satisfy yourself that it will do the job you want it for. I'm hopeful that the ProMix will herald a new era in semi-pro mixers, not because it's digital, but because it has brought motorised faders down to an all-time low price, which might just signal the end of VCA automation.

MULTI-TRACK RECORDER TYPES

Ignoring some of the hyper-expensive true-pro gear (like DASH), there are really just four main types of multi-track recorder: analogue on Compact Cassette, analogue on open reel, digital on video cassette, and digital on hard (computer) disk.

Tascam MSR-16S: like Fostex G16S, offers 16-track recording on half-inch tape

ANALOGUE

This simply means that what is recorded is analogous to the original signal, which in turn is just a fancy way of saying that the magnetic field on tape gets stronger when the input signal is louder, and weaker when the input is quieter. Unfortunately though, real-world practice isn't quite this straightforward.

The tape itself will have some low-level random magnetism on it, and this translates into noise/hiss. And at the high-level end, too much signal produces overload or tape-saturation distortion – you can pile on more signal, but the tape is already fully-magnetised, so the signal peaks just get 'chopped', which is audibly nasty. Even before we reach this drastic point, there's a little number called 'tape squash' to consider. Record a constant tone at, say, -10dB, and you'd quite reasonably expect it to play back at -10dB. But try the same trick at maybe +6dB, and you'll find that the playback signal comes out a couple of dBs lower than expected – the tape has 'squashed' the strength of the signal.

In an ideal world, the tape would travel at an absolutely constant speed, but in reality, there are short-term speed variations caused, for example, by the inevitably less-than-perfect machining of components like the drive capstan. These variations are collectively known as wow and flutter, where wow refers to relatively slowly-changing speed errors, and flutter to much faster/shorter-lived errors. The audible effects can be quite obvious, even when the testbench specs seem good. A reasonable ballpark figure might be 0.1percent, and since 0.1percent equals one part in a thousand, you might suppose that a mid-frequency tone of, say, 1000Hz, would only be changed by just 1Hz – surely inaudible? Well, no. To show up wow, try some slow piano music, which can reveal a kind of 'drunken' wavering in pitch, while flutter is easily demonstrated by acoustic guitar, which acquires an unpleasant 'gargling' effect.

Analogue recording has other problems, such as 'modulation noise', where background hiss rises and falls along with changes in signal level, 'crosstalk', which is 'leakage' between tracks, and signal 'drop-outs', particularly on the tracks nearest the edges of the tape.

NOISE REDUCTION

The difference between low-level noise and high-level distortion is known as dynamic range, and is expressed in dBs (see *A Quick Tour*). As a guide, a mid-price cassette deck might have a basic dynamic range of 50dB, a pro-quality open-reeler maybe 65dB. Both of these figures are far less than the potential dynamic range of music (around 90dB), which means that when we turn the wick up, tape noise is going to be clearly audible. What can we do?

Well, short of changing to a 'better' recorder or tape, all we can do is adapt the signal itself to make the most of the dynamic range that's available. The idea here is quite straightforward: during the recording process, we reduce or compress the signal's dynamic range, then, on playback, we restore or expand it.

Let's take the case of **dbx** noise reduction, which uses 2:1 compression when recording, and its complement, 1:2 expansion, during playback. This means that if our original signal has a dynamic range of 90dB, we compress it into just 45dB as the signal goes to tape, then expand the off-tape signal back to its original 90dB. Since 45dB is well within the dynamic range of even fairly basic cassette decks, hiss is banished completely. Or is it?

Under some circumstances, dbx (no capitals because that's the way

Tascam 488: one of many cassette multi-trackers with 'standard' dbx noise reduction

dbx Inc like it) certainly does do the business, for example in the way it provides almost complete silence during inter-track breaks. But, particularly with cassette decks, there can be some very real problems at other times. Let's take an especially nasty case: a bass drum recorded at a sensible level, say -6dB. Talking very generally, the dbx system does virtually nothing to this signal – it doesn't get compressed much during recording, and it doesn't get expanded much on playback. So, as we listen to the tape, there's the expected virtual silence before the drum beat; but then, as the signal level comes up, so does the tape noise, and we hear it, sometimes as out-and-out hiss, sometimes as a roughness in the sound. The bass drum example is especially effective at revealing this sort of naughtiness, because our ears and brains can easily distinguish deep bass signal from treble hiss. But the roughness effect is also quite audible on mainly mid-frequency sounds such as piano and voice – just the frequencies the ear/brain is most sensitive to.

What we're dealing with here is known as 'noise modulation', so-called because the noise modulates (alters and varies with) the signal itself. If you test-drive a dbx four-track, particularly on single instruments, listening at a decent level in a quiet environment, and you don't hear those unpleasant effects, then there's something fairly seriously wrong with whatever gear you're listening through. Or your ears. It really is as simple as that. (Note, though, that dbx can work quite well with open-reel recorders, partly because they generally have a better dynamic range to begin with, therefore there's less noise to show up, but also because open-reel dbx works slightly differently.)

For reasons I don't fully understand, dbx has become almost the standard in multi-track cassette noise reduction – perhaps it's a combination of that marvellous inter-track silence and the paper-spec of a 90+dB dynamic range. But Dolby Labs offer several alternative noise reduction systems.

The simplest of these is the classic **Dolby B**, as found on just about every hi-fi cassette deck, many Walkies, and all pre-recorded cassettes. As with dbx, the basic idea is to record with compression, then play back with expansion, but Dolby B takes a much more subtle approach. It ignores bass and midrange signals, and concentrates only on the treble. As the level here drops, it boosts the treble range by up to 10dB – a form of mild high-frequency compression. Then, on playback, it reverses the process, restoring the treble to its original level and, at the same time, cutting hiss by up to 10dB. This relatively gentle manipulation of the signal means there are far fewer side-effects (noise modulation) than dbx, but 10dB of noise reduction isn't all that much – hiss will still be audible at high playback levels.

To address this limitation, Dolby introduced their **Dolby C** noise reduction system. Simplifying so appallingly that I can only justify it on the grounds that we don't have space to spare, Dolby C not only uses as much as double the low-level compression and expansion, but also varies the frequency range it works on according to the make-up of the signal. Together, these techniques give up to 20dB of noise reduction. This is a much more realistic proposition for serious recording, and a Dolby C cassette is almost as quiet as dbx on the old inter-track test. But the really good news is that, largely because of this 'sliding frequency' approach, noise modulation still isn't much of a problem – there's a slight dulling of transients, and an equally slight loss

Fostex 380S is equipped with Dolby S, the best noise reduction for budget multi-tracking

of 'transparency', as if a thin veil is obscuring clarity, but these effects are fairly easy to live with.

The latest arrival from Dolby is the **Dolby S** system, a simplified version of their professional **SR** (Spectral Recording) noise reduction, itself promoted as analogue's answer to digital. Dolby S builds on C's principles of combining different (and sliding) frequency bands with variable compansion, delivering improved paper-specs and considerable overall audible improvements. Dolby S is currently probably the best choice for 'affordable' analogue multi-tracking, though C isn't dramatically far behind and, on cassette, either can comfortably beat dbx. Which brings us to...

COMPACT CASSETTE & OPEN REEL

Without getting overly technical, the basic point is that potential analogue sound quality improves as you do two things: run the tape faster, and make each recording track wider. Between them, these two measures bring several benefits: reduced wow and flutter, reduced hiss, reduced distortion, and more extended treble response, especially at high recording levels. To put it another way: better sound all round.

At one extreme we have ordinary cassettes running at 1⅞ips (inches per second), and with a track width of just over half a millimetre. At the other, pro open-reelers racing along at 16times that speed, with a track width about three times greater. Between the two, we find things like high-speed cassette, eight-track high-speed cassette, and open-reelers like the Fostex R8 and G16S, with 15ips tape speed, but tracks no wider than standard cassette.

There are no prizes for guessing that, in very general terms, the higher the quality, the higher the price. But whether cassette or open-reel, the formats we've been looking at are collectively known as 'narrow-gauge', which in turn refers not only to the track width (compared with 'true-pro' 16/24 on two-inch tape), but also to the gaps between tracks, known as 'guard bands'.

Narrow-gauge is particularly prone to the crosstalk and dropout problems I mentioned earlier. Crosstalk often doesn't matter in practice, but two circumstances can be real swines. One occurs where a deep bass track is erased/changed, yet the original magnetic signal has leaked across the guard band, so that the crosstalk lingers on adjacent tracks, even after the original track has gone. The other is when you're using a track for timecode or sync – though not bassy, this 'demented-Morse-Code-wasp' noise crosstalks a treat. In cassette-based systems, we're not usually expecting to play back at levels that will reveal the crosstalk, so most users aren't troubled; but people pushing narrow-gauge (or even full-gauge) to the limits, will often find they need to leave an unused 'guard track' between code and audio. By common practice, code goes to the highest-numbered track, so on an eight-track, code is on 8 and guard is 7, rather importantly leaving only six tracks for audio. Using an outside track makes sense, in that it means we need only one guard track, but it also makes the code vulnerable to the dropout problem mentioned earlier. This can be a Right Sod, because when you lose sync, you also lose everything that's running off the sync. Interestingly, this isn't usually a problem with cassette, and if it happens on open-reel tape, it may be caused by the reel, or by uneven 'tape-packing' during fast wind.

'Separate' recorders can always record on any or all tracks at the same time, but some four-tracks have limitations here – budget models may be able to record only on two tracks at once, while most eight-tracks can record only four (and you don't have a free choice of which four – you have to choose from odd/even pairs, as in 1/5, 2/6, 3/7, 4/8). This could be an important aspect if you want to record a whole band in a single take, most obviously in live performances.

TRANSPORT FEATURES

The sophistication or otherwise of their transport systems is a major consideration when considering tape machines, and it is an area in which wide variation may be found from model to model. At the very bottom end of the market, I've seen budget four-tracks that don't even have auto-stop on fast wind; a more subtle version of this is where you leave the pause button down, then fast wind – on some machines, using pause effectively disables the autostop. The first step up in transport features is the incredibly simple, but incredibly useful, 'stop at zero' fast-wind function – almost essential for rewinding to the start of a track.

The biggest transport feature on mid-price four-tracks and up is 'soft-touch' operation. In itself, this doesn't mean a lot, but once all the tape-handling mechanisms are power-driven, it becomes possible to use a small onboard computer to do all sorts of clever things. The first is to provide multiple tape position memories (for example, at various points within a track you're working on), plus of course, the ability to fast-wind to any of these positions. By using two memories together, a recorder can create a 'loop' function, repeatedly playing and rewinding a specific section of tape. This is most commonly used to practice drop-ins, and is often catered for with a 'rehearsal' mode, that includes automatic switching between tape and source at the appropriate point. Other refinements include 'real-time' tape counters and remote control; with open-reel recorders it is useful to be able to set 'beginning' and 'end' markers, so the tape doesn't fly off the reels when fast-winding.

DIGITAL

The ideas involved in digital recording can get very, very complicated, but all we really need to deal with here are two concepts: bit-resolution and sample rates. To understand bit-resolution, think in terms of an ordinary calculator – one with, say, ten digits is always going to produce more accurate results than one with only six digits (except on simple stuff like 2 + 2). Digital audio measures the strength of the signal at a particular moment in time, and

Alesis ADAT: uses S-VHS video cassettes to give 40 minutes of digital recording time

converts it into numbers – the greater the number of digits or bits used, the more accurate the measurement can be. Some early digital gear used only 12 or 14 bits; today the norm is 16, and state-of-the-art gear uses 20, 22, or even 24 bits.

Sample rate is just techno-talk for how often the recorder makes its signal-strength measurements. CD sample rate is 44,100 times a second (44.1kHz), while digital recorders can work at 44.1 or 48kHz, and some really advanced stuff operates at 96kHz. Sample rates have several effects on sound quality, but by far the most important is that the rate determines the treble frequency response – without delving into the theory, the maximum frequency response will always be slightly less than half the sample rate, so that CD for example extends to just over 20kHz. It's tempting to think that this is all one could possibly need, since it is generally accepted that human hearing dies around the 20kHz mark. But experience strongly suggests that this isn't the whole story – lots of people have had the opportunity to confirm this for themselves, thanks to Pioneer's D-07 high-speed DAT recorder, which runs at 96kHz (treble response to around 45kHz), and consistently sounds better than any conventional 44.1 or 48kHz DAT.

In terms of paper-spec performance, there's little to choose between the various digital multi-track formats, with a dynamic range of around 90dB, distortion about a hundred times lower than analogue, and effectively complete absence of wow and flutter. Crosstalk is also vastly reduced, and timecode has its own separate track.

VIDEO CASSETTE & HARD DISK
Video recorders have long been used for digital audio recording, and there are two current multi-track formats based on this technology: ADAT from Alesis

and Fostex, and Hi-8 from Tascam. Both systems provide eight audio tracks plus timecode; ADAT uses S-VHS cassettes to give 40 minutes recording time, while Hi-8 rather unsurprisingly uses Hi-8 cassettes, as designed for camcorders, and provides 100 minutes recording time (this last fact could be important if you intend using your multi-track to record live gigs).

Both formats are proving popular, and experience to date suggests that you can safely base your choice on the features you want – it seems there's really nothing to choose in sound quality or reliability. ADAT and Hi-8 work out to about twice the cost-per-track of, say, narrow-gauge analogue on a fostex R8, so there will doubtless continue to be healthy demand for the latter into the foreseeable future. But, in the minds of many buyers, the really important point about both ADAT and Hi-8 is that they're expandable – assuming you can afford to think digital in the first place, you can start with just the basic eight tracks, then upgrade to 16 or even more when funds permit, and without junking your original recorder.

Recording on hard disk (which is like a floppy disk, but much faster and with far more memory) has long been regarded as a desirable goal. The two principal attractions are near-instant access (no spooling delays), and the potential, with suitable software, for non-destructive editing, which combines a near-infinite number of different mixes and edits with the ability to 'undo' things when they don't work out or go wrong. Also, on a hard 'n' soft package, you can expect to find lots of sampler-type facilities, such as looping, time-compression and stretch – none of which is really surprising, since a hard-disk recorder is essentially just a giant sampler.

One practical drawback of hard disk is that most disk-drives are 'fixed' – the equivalent of a tape recorder where you can't change tapes. This can be a real nuisance when you want to work on several different songs at once – you can buy equipment to copy or 'back-up' the disk to, say, DAT, but it's a painfully slow process, and just as slow when you want to reload the data onto your disk. Another very real problem with hard disk is price. The culprit here is a combination of the need for computing power and speed, plus the price of the disk-drive itself. Digital audio consumes memory at an alarming rate: over five megabytes per track per minute – that's more than 400mbytes for an eight-track, ten-minute song. It also requires what's called a 'fast-access' disk-drive, where 'fast-access' equals more money. If you're going to make use of hard disk's special features (typically in dance music), then you'll find it unbeatable, but for many purposes, hard disk still can't compete head-to-head with tape-based systems. A dealer friend summarises the current situation thus: "Hard disk is getting there, but it's not there yet".

MULTI-TRACK RECORDER MODELS

Akai DR4: established hard-disk recorder with simultaneous recording on all four tracks

AKAI DR4 – £1500

Well-established hard-disk recorder, now facing competition from Vestax. The basic price excludes the disk-drive itself – a 250mb SCSI drive will add around £400. Though possibly of limited appeal, the Akai's trump card over the Vestax HDR4/6 machines (see below) is that it provides simultaneous recording on all four tracks. An eight-track version, the DR8, has been announced but at press time, was not shipping or priced – vapourware.

ALESIS ADAT – £4,000

Best-seller of the digital-on-video machines, the Alesis ADAT is ready-to-roll as a basic recorder, but needs (extra-cost) add-ons for syncing or MIDI machine control. These extras will probably push the total price up to around the level of the Fostex RD-8, where most interfaces are included as standard.

Alesis ADAT: best selling digital-on-video machine, but check out the Fostex RD-8 too

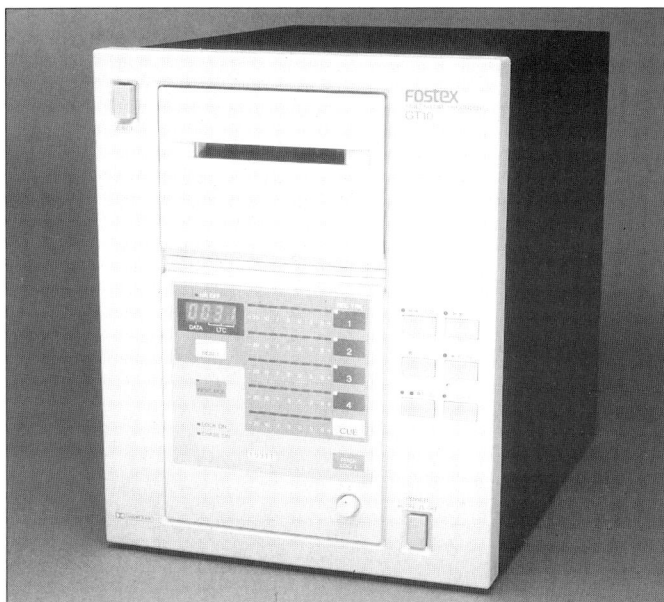

Fostex GT-10: cassette recorder designed for the MIDI user

FOSTEX GT-10 – £1000

Cassette-based four-track recorders, without integral mixer and usually rackmountable, have been around for many years, notably from Tascam. Those who use 'em love 'em, but in volume terms, the UK market is minuscule. The GT-10 is an attempt to update the concept with one particular kind of application/user in mind – the MIDI environment. The 10's features are attractive, with high-speed Dolby S and, very importantly, a fifth dedicated timecode track. This can be used for MIDI timecode, although the machine actually uses the professional SMPTE system internally. As you'd expect of a MIDI-orientated machine, it can run under MIDI machine control from a suitable sequencer. If you're happy with cassette quality, and want total MIDI integration, or audio-video sync via SMPTE, the GT-10 could be just what you need, but we're talking about a specialist product, and it seems to me that the price-tag reflects this somewhat.

FOSTEX R8 – £1880

Fostex pretty much single-handedly popularised the 'narrow-gauge' 8-on-¼in format, combining it with the cost savings of catering only for seven-inch tape reels (giving the same 22½ minute record time as high-speed cassette). Excellent metering and transport controls are both on a removable 'keyboard-size' remote, an operational delight. Dolby C, though not as sexy as S, performs well here – sound quality is in a completely different league from any cassette-based multi-track, and entirely up to release standard for all but the most difficult types of music.

Popular Fostex open-reelers: above, R8; below, G16S

FOSTEX G16S – £6000

Running 16 tracks on half-inch tape is equivalent to the R8's 8-on-¼in format, but this time with 10½in reels and Dolby S. Again, metering and transport are remotable as standard, so again, an operational delight. Sound quality is a smidgen clearer than the R 8's, presumably down to Dolby S over C.

Fostex G24S: offers budget-priced 24-track recording on one inch tape

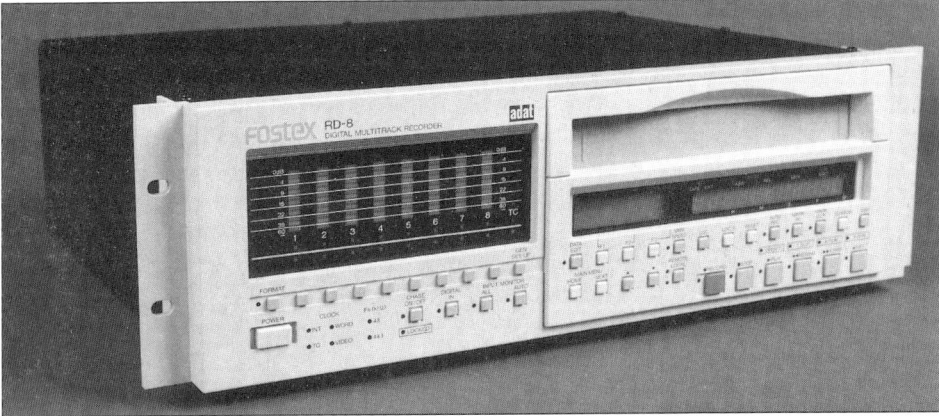

Fostex RD-8: basically ADAT with knobs on – but make sure you need all its facilities

FOSTEX G24S – £8000

Take a G16, add eight tracks and two thousand pounds, and you've got a G24 – note that this uses one inch tape rather than the 16's half inch, which immediately doubles your running costs compared with the 16-track version. 24-on-1 gives a larger track-width than 16-on-½in, but I doubt if you'll really notice the sound quality gains in practice.

FOSTEX RD-8 – £4560

This is ADAT with knobs, or to be more precise, sockets, on. Offering just about every kind of sync and control you could imagine as standard, the resulting price makes sense if you'll use these facilities – equally, it's questionable whether you'd want to pay the premium if you're putting together a 16/24-track ADAT set-up, 'cos you'll be paying needlessly to duplicate these features.

TASCAM TSR-8 – £2300

For around 20 percent more than the Fostex R8, Tascam give you 10½in reels, true-pro 8-on-½in format, and dbx instead of Dolby. In theory, the wider track format delivers higher quality, but this is complicated by the differences between dbx and Dolby, and there's also the point that with twice the tape width, your running costs will be twice as high. Shame it doesn't have the same 'free' remote that the R8 offers.

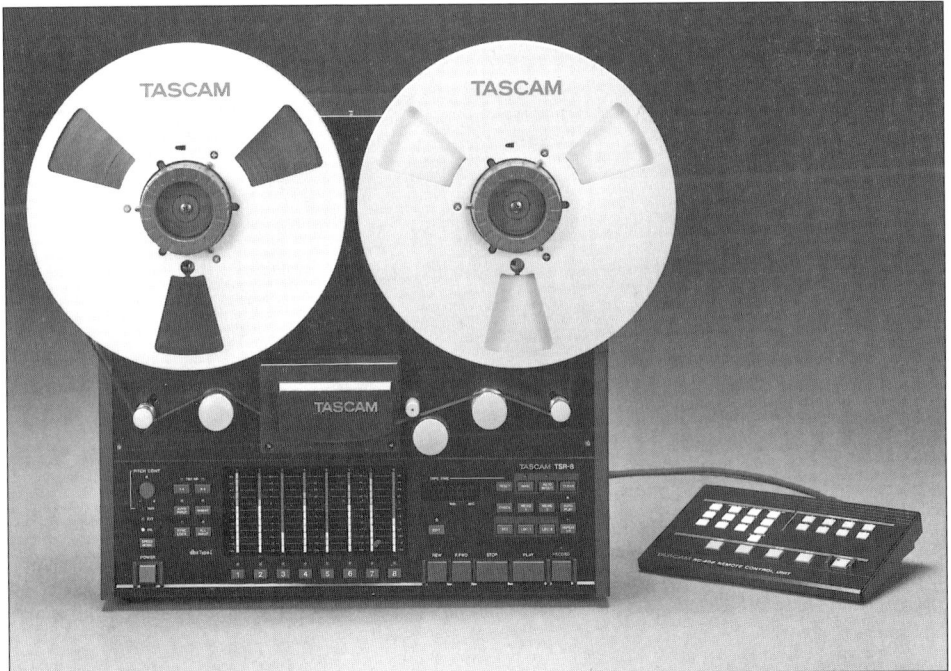

Tascam TSR-8: true-pro 8-on-½in format and 10½in reels, but dbx instead of Dolby

Tascam MSR-16S (above) and MSR-24S (below): Dolby S, but remote control is extra

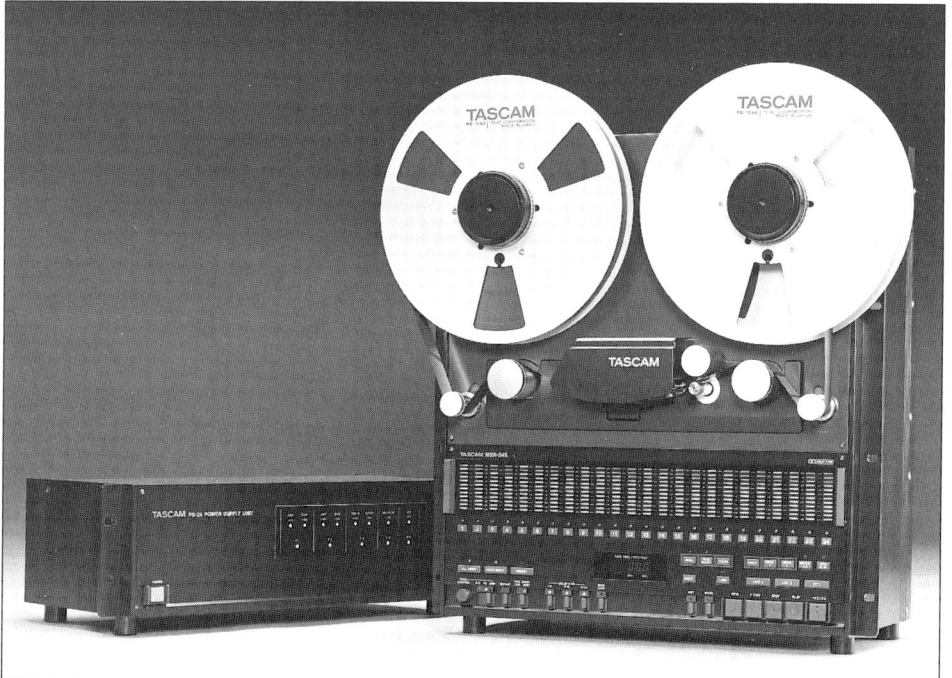

TASCAM MSR-16 – £5000/MSR-16S – £6000

With different but comparable features to the Fostex G16S, you can have the Tascam with dbx for £800 less, or the Dolby S version for exactly the same price. Depending on how you'll be working, the lack of remotable controls as standard may count against the Tascam.

TASCAM MSR-24 – £8500/MSR-24S – £10,000

As you'd expect, the basic 24 is dbx and the 24S is Dolby S. One inch tape replace the 16-on-½in format, with a doubling of tape costs and a (very) slight performance improvement. Still no remote-as-standard.

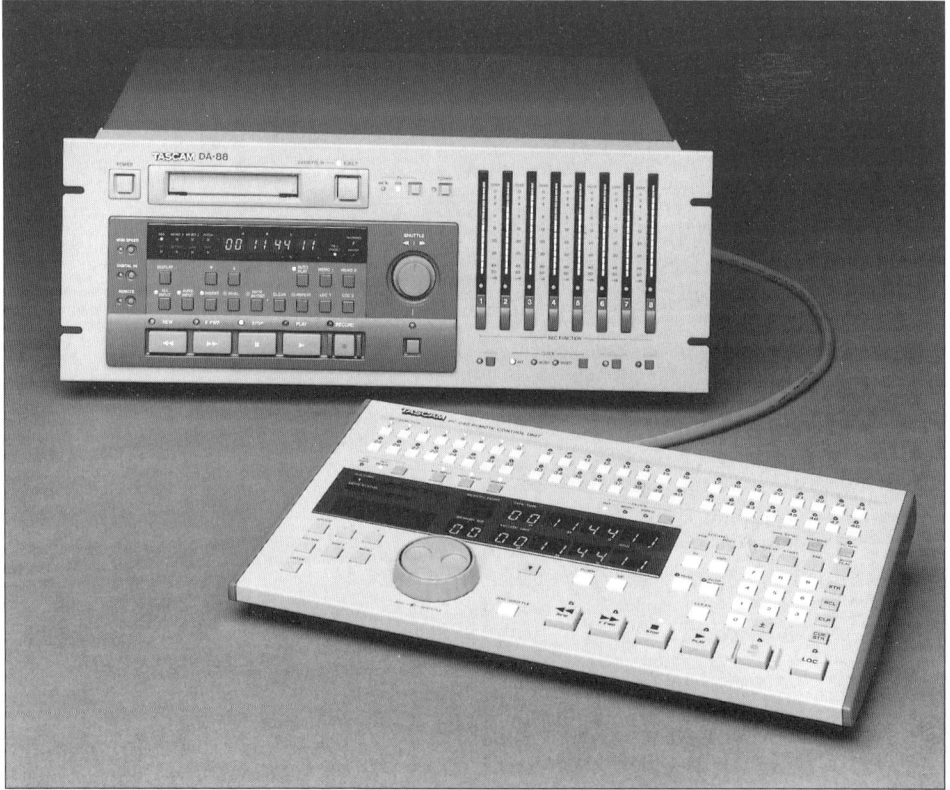

Tascam DA-88: continuous recording time of 113 minutes on Hi-8 video cassette

TASCAM DA-88 – £4000

Tascam's Hi-8 format beats ADAT on continuous recording time (113 versus 40 minutes), provides faster tape handling, and offers a 'jog'/'shuttle' dial (probably not much use in ordinary music recording, but excellent for any form of audio-for-video). Only basic syncability as standard, but loads of options, and internal construction is highly modular, which could make servicing easier.

VESTAX MR-66 – £1,195

A casual glance might suggest that this high-speed, dbx, six-track cassette recorder belongs in Portastudio territory, but though it looks like there's a mixer, it turns out that you can't actually mix different inputs together and send them to a single track. This might be fine for some ways of working, but falls way below the mix capabilities of just about any portable multi-track. Comparisons with the eight-track, mixer-inclusive Yamaha MT-8X, at £100 less, are inevitable, and it seems to me that the only way the Vestax wins is that it can record six tracks simultaneously, as opposed to the Yamaha's four.

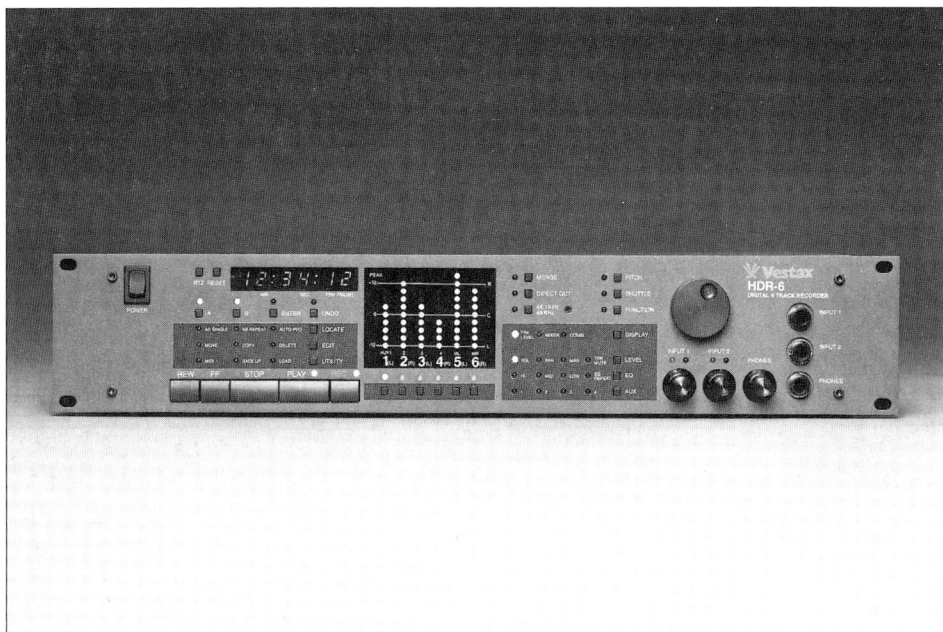

Vestax HDR-4: DR4 competitor has digital mixer but can record only two-tracks at once

VESTAX HDR-4 – £1795/HDR-6 – £1995

Offering four or six tracks, respectively with 250 or 320mb disks built-in, the standard HDR-4/6 can record only two tracks at once, but this can be increased with an add-on analogue-digital board, the price of which still hadn't been announced at press time. Pitching against the Akai DR4, the Vestax's key point is that it includes a digital mixer, with three-band EQ (mid sweep), plus effect sends and returns. If such a basic mixer will meet your needs, then the Vestax machines look strong value-for-money.

MULTI-TRACK CASSETTE SYSTEMS

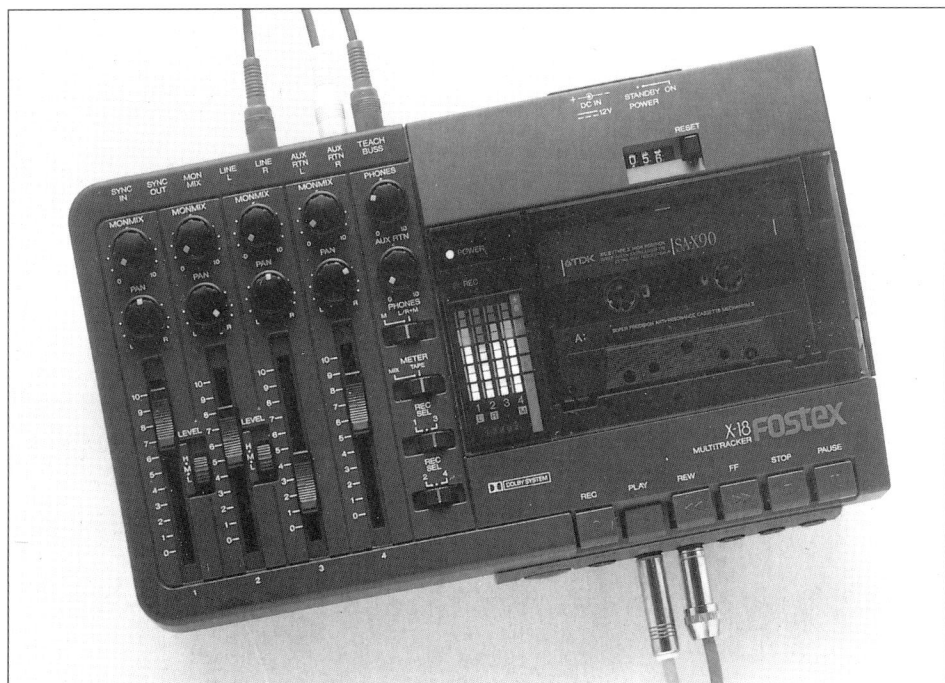

Fostex X-18: basic machine at a very basic price; another £30 buys the high-speed X-18H

The integrated four-track cassette recorder and mixer was invented in around 1979 by the Japanese firm Teac, and launched under their professional brand of Tascam. They called it the Portastudio, a name now widely used by musicians as the general term for all portable multi-track cassette recorders, in much the same way that people tend to call all vacuum cleaners Hoovers. In this book, however, the term Portastudio is used only to describe genuine Tascam products.

Chief among Tascam's rivals in the multi-track cassette recorder market is Fostex, a firm set up by ex-Tascam people who split from the parent company in the early eighties. Today these two high profile brands between them have the biggest share of the market, while other players in the field include Marantz, Vestax and Yamaha.

Beginning below, in alphabetical order of manufacturer, are brief descriptions and comments on 17 four- and eight-track machines, ranging in price from just under £300 to nearly £2500.

FOSTEX X-18 – £309
Standard-speed with Dolby B, the X-18 can only record on two tracks at once. Four inputs, two with three-position switches to do the same job as a trim control, the other two being line only. There's no effect send as such, but the monitor mix controls have a back-panel output, so at mixdown time they can be used as a send – a stereo return is provided. No EQ at all, and no master fader, so fadeouts will have to be done with the volume control on your stereo deck.

FOSTEX X-18H – £339
Identical to the X-18, except that the £30 extra buys you the high-speed version – well worth it for sound quality, but note that the X-18H is high-speed only.

Fostex X-28H: dual-speed machine with eight inputs and other useful features

FOSTEX X-28H – £449
Dual-speed with Dolby B, eight inputs (four mike/line) all with effect send, and soft-touch controls with zero-stop and a rehearsal mode. No channel EQ, but two-band on the stereo buss when recording or mixing down.

FOSTEX 280 – £699
High-speed only with Dolby C. Four mike/line inputs with three-band EQ

Fostex 280: features include high-speed operation, Dolby C and multiple memories

(sweep mid), two sends (one switchable pre/post), but one of the sends is used for the track monitor mix. Four line-only inputs, with a single effect send. Multiple memories with auto drop-in/out. Transport functions can be MIDI-controlled via an MTC1 interface, but this costs a whopping £289 extra.

Fostex 380S: flagship model with Dolby S and mixer section offering up to 12 live inputs

AT THESE PRICES YOU'D BE MAD TO BUY ONE

(YOU SHOULD BUY AT LEAST TWO)

MK 219
£265
+ VAT

MK 012
£300
+ VAT

Introducing the Oktava MK 219 and MK 012 high quality studio condenser microphones, manufactured in Russia and now available here in the UK at list prices that wouldn't even cover the VAT on similar performance models.

The Oktava MK 012 is a high quality capacitor microphone which utilises interchangeable capsules making it suitable in any situation where an accurate sound is required.

"You get a lot of mic for your money when you buy Oktava." CHRIS KEMPSTER (The Mix)

"They're amazing value at £300!" SIMON EADON (Recording engineer)

The Oktava MK 219 is a fixed pattern, cardioid condenser microphone which employs a large, gold plated diaphragm built to a classic design, enabling it to outperform models many times its price.

"The Oktava really is unbeatable for its price." DAVID ETHERIDGE (Music Mart)

"You could easily pay twice the asking price for this mic, or even more, and still not improve on the sound." PAUL WHITE (Sound on Sound)

DISTRIBUTED BY

A.S. McKay Ltd., 6 Bridle Close, Surbiton Road, Kingston upon Thames, Surrey KT1 2JW Tel 081 541 1177 Fax 081 546 2779

AND AVAILABLE THROUGH THE FOLLOWING STOCKISTS

Music Lab	London	071 388 5392
Misc Co	Brighton	0273 552985
Digital Village	London	081 440 3440
Sound Control	Scotland	041 204 0322
Dawsons Music	Cheshire	0925 632591
Music Corp	Ringwood	0425 470007

Oktava

NICE ONE COMRADE

FOSTEX 380S – £799

Flagship Fostex, boasting Dolby S and a mixer section that offers up to 12 live inputs plus tape tracks. The first four inputs are mike/line, and two of these have XLR sockets (no phantom) and insert points. EQ on these four channels is three-band with sweep mid, and there is in-line monitoring with a 'flip' capability, effectively adding a further four inputs. There are then eight line inputs, configured as four stereo pairs. The aux/effect arrangements may seem complicated at first sight, partly because one of the two sends acts as the monitor mix for virtual tracks, but also because the stereo inputs have a single control for both sends, so you can't use both at once. Still, at least you can send any of the 16 channels to a reverb or whatever. Multiple memories with a rehearsal mode and auto drop-in/out. On the downside, although the 380S is dual-speed, Dolby S works only on high-speed, which makes standard-speed pretty useless.

MARANTZ PMD-720 – £549

Dual-speed with dbx, the 720 certainly looks The Biz, and in many ways is a joy to use, chiefly because it's relatively large for the number of controls, which makes it easy to drive. Four mike/line inputs, two with XLRs (no phantom) and inserts, and two-band EQ. Four line inputs arranged as two stereo pairs, but no effect send on these channels. Soft-touch transport, but only a basic stop-at-zero facility. Annoyingly, the meters are virtually useless tiny moving-needle types.

Marantz PMD-740: dual speed, dbx and Dolby HX Pro, plus XLRs on four of the inputs

MARANTZ PMD-740 – £699

According to the sales bumf, the 740 is 'built by rocket scientists', a concept I find as fascinating as it is improbable. Dual-speed with dbx, the 740 is the only portable with Dolby HX Pro. This isn't a noise reduction system, but a clever little gizmo that reduces the amount of tape squash at high frequencies by up to 6dB. There are six mike/line inputs, and four of them have XLRs (no phantom) and insert points, with three-band EQ including sweep mid and a wide/narrow Q switch. The remaining two mike/line channels have just simple two-band EQ, plus effect send. There's a stereo line in with a fiddly level control on the back panel, and two separate phones outputs. Multiple memory points support rehearsal and auto drop-in/out. Silly moving-needle meters with green/red back-lighting to indicate record status – the 'rocket scientists' got this seriously wrong, because the lamps only change to red when the tape actually starts rolling – a bit late to realise you've selected the wrong track.

Tascam Porta 07: high speed but basic dbx Porta which records only two tracks at once

TASCAM PORTA 07 – £399

High-speed only, with dbx, and you can only record on two tracks at once. Four inputs, two with mike/line trim, and all with two-band EQ and effect send. There's also a stereo buss in, but no level control or effect send on this.

TASCAM 424 – £549

Comes with dbx and three speeds, including a half-speed option, the only

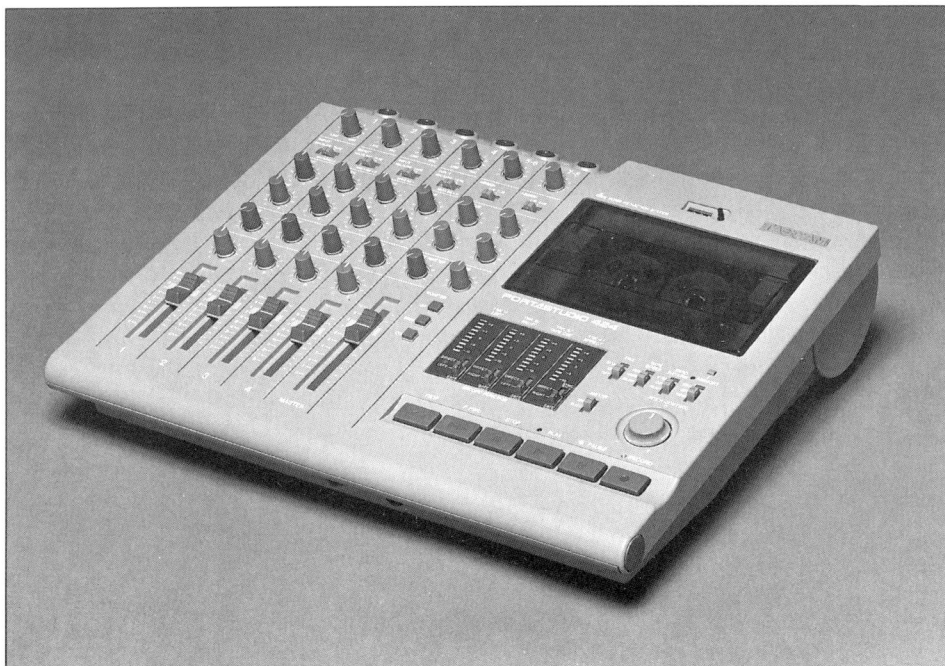

Tascam 424: dbx and three tape speeds, plus effective provision of up to 12 channels

conceivable use for which would be to help you analyse fast guitar riffs and such. Four mike/line inputs, with two-band EQ and an effect send, plus four line inputs arranged as two stereo pairs, but no effect send on these. The four main inputs can be used at the same time as playing back tape tracks, giving a total of twelve channels/tracks, but there's no effect return as such, so you'll need to use a stereo pair for this. Soft-touch transport with two memory positions and optional auto-play, but no rehearsal facilities.

TASCAM 464 – £799
Dual-speed with dbx, the 464 has four mike/line inputs with XLRs (no phantom), and inserts on channels 1 and 2. Three-band EQ with sweep mid, and two effect sends. Eight line inputs arranged as four stereo pairs, two with two-band EQ and two effect sends, the others with just level controls. The four main inputs can be used while playing back tape tracks, so you could have a total of 16 channels/tracks, but two of the inputs will be needed to act as a stereo effect return. Soft-touch controls provide multiple memories, rehearsal and auto drop-in/out. LCD metering needs a bright working environment.

TASCAM 644 MIDISTUDIO – £999
Dual-speed with dbx, eight mike/line inputs, all with inserts, and two with XLRs (no phantom). Three-band EQ with sweep mid, and two sends (one selectable pre/post). There are then eight further line inputs, four of which do

Tascam 644 Midistudio: inbuilt MIDI-FSK converter and computer-memorised settings

double duty as track monitors. LCD meters need good lighting. Multiple memories provide rehearsal and auto drop-in/out, and there's a shuttle control for fine tape positioning. The two big features on this machine are a built-in MIDI-FSK converter, plus automation of channel inputs, mutes, group assigns, and effect return assigns. The onboard computer can store 99 'snapshots' (Tascam call them 'scenes') of all these settings, and you can then select them either manually, or from an external MIDI device such as a sequencer.

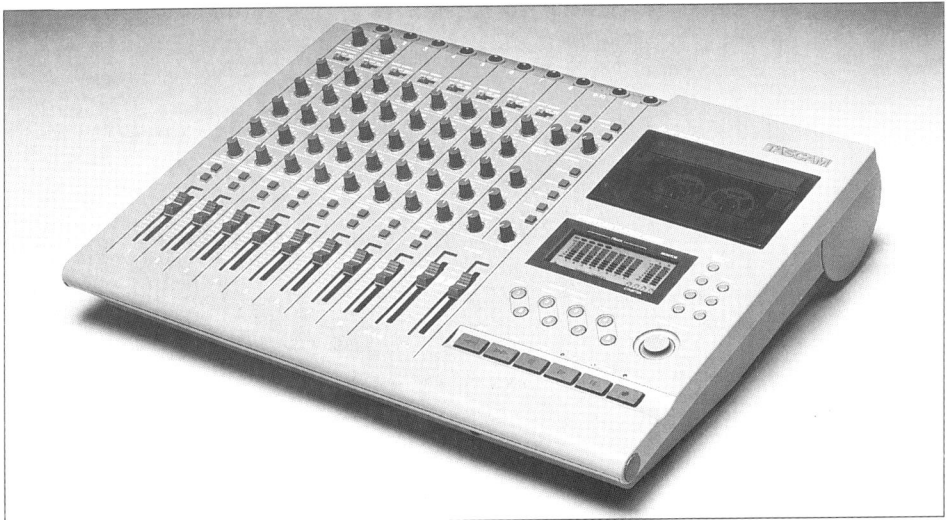

Tascam 488: high speed dbx eight-tracker, but records only on four tracks at once

TASCAM 488 – £1499

Eight-track with dbx and high-speed only, but you can record only on four tracks at once. Eight main inputs (but only two with mike/line trim), two-band EQ, and two sends. These inputs can be used at the same time as playing tape tracks, and there are two stereo inputs, one of which will normally be used as an effect return. Multiple memories with rehearsal but not auto drop-in/out. LCD metering needs good illumination.

Tascam 688 Midistudio: only cassette machine with simultaneous eight-track recording

TASCAM 688 MIDISTUDIO – £2499

Eight-track with dbx and high-speed only, the 688 – unlike other cassette eight-tracks – can record on all eight tracks at once. Ten mike/line inputs, all with XLRs (no phantom), inserts, three-band EQ with sweep mid, and two sends (one switchable pre/post), plus a further ten line-only inputs. Unlike the 644, these are usable at all times, because there's a separate monitor mix section. Transport, MIDI and automation are all as on the 644, and the flash-looking meter bridge comes as standard (as it jolly well should at this price).

VESTAX MR-300 – £296

At just £13 less than the Fostex X-18, the MR-300 is the cheapest four-track in town – and quite possibly the weirdest. Standard-speed with Dolby B, it

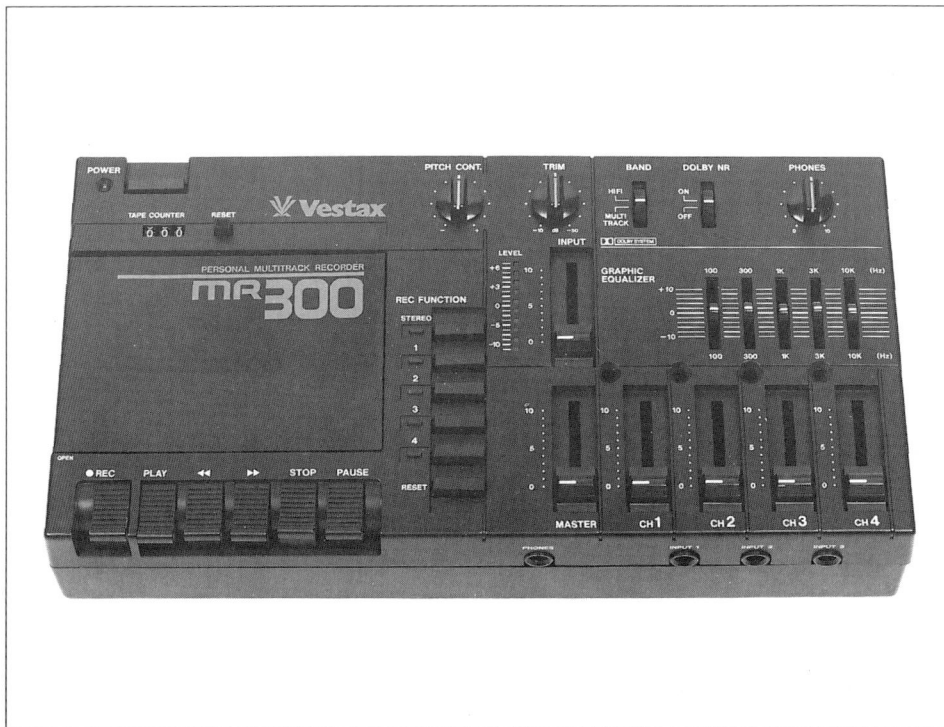

Vestax MR-300: the cheapest four-track in town – and quite possibly the weirdest

seems from a quick glance to have just a single input with mike/line trim, but there are also two front-panel line inputs without any form of level control – this shouldn't be a problem with gear like keyboards, since they'll have their own volume controls. These three inputs are mixed together and fed to whichever track you're recording on. You can also record on two tracks at once, using the strangely-named 'band' switch – this places the three front-panel inputs equally on tracks 1 and 2, also using two rear-panel phono line inputs to feed the two tracks individually. Note that, for reasons I don't pretend to understand, you can't monitor track 3 while recording on track 4.

Come mixdown time, you discover that the pan controls are silly little recessed presets that can only be altered with a screwdriver. (A *screwdriver?*) There's a five-band mini-graphic EQ but, quite amazingly, this can't be used when recording tracks, only on the final stereo mix. No effect facilities.

VESTAX MR-44 – £549
Dual-speed with dbx, the MR-44 is rack-mountable – this could be a useful plus point, but bear in mind that with a 'normal' rack, the faders will be vertical, and this is going to make operation rather tricky. Four mike/line inputs, a single effect send with stereo return, no channel EQ, but a stereo

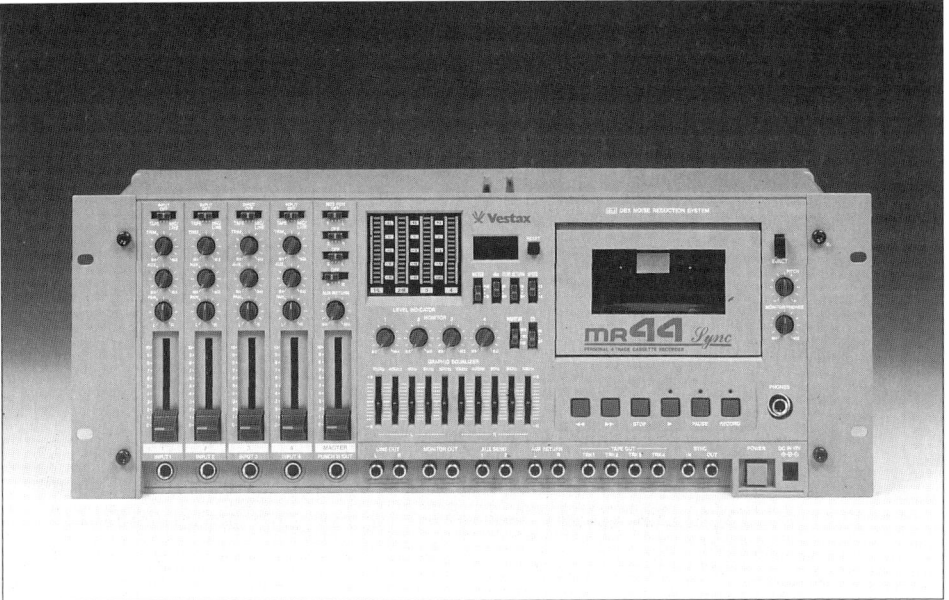

Vestax MR44: rack-mountable, with two speeds, dbx and stereo five-band graphic

five-band mini-graphic that can be used when recording through the stereo buss, and on the final stereo mix. Soft-touch controls, but only stop-at-zero. Almost unbelievably, the power-in socket is on the front panel.

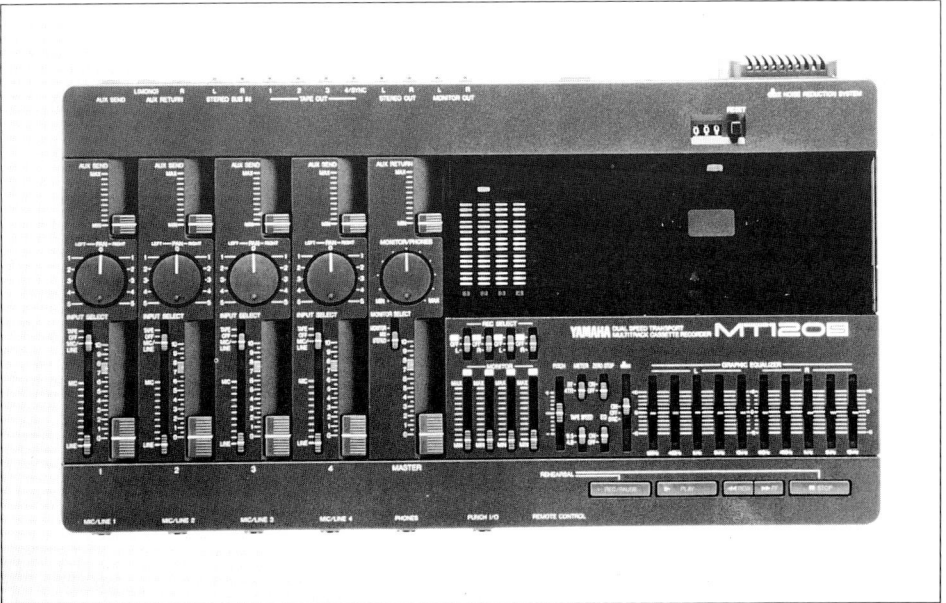

Yamaha MT120S: dual-speed with dbx and a smoked plastic panel obscuring the LEDs

YAMAHA MT120S – £499

Dual-speed with dbx, the 120S features four mike/line inputs, but no XLRs or inserts. There is no channel EQ as such, but a stereo five-band mini-graphic can be used if you're recording via the stereo buss, or during mixdown. Effect send with stereo return, and stereo buss inputs. Soft-touch controls, but only basic zero-stop. An extra £39 buys you a remote control for transport functions. In a victory of style over sense, the LED meters are covered by a smoked plastic panel, specially designed to make them hard to read...

Yamaha MT8X: high speed, eight tracks and dbx, but only records on four tracks at once

YAMAHA MT8X – £1199

Eight-track recorder with dbx and high-speed alone, but note that you can only record on four tracks at once. Four mike/line inputs (no XLRs, but channels 1 and 2 have insert points), with input-clip LEDs, three-band EQ (fixed mid), and two effect sends. Three further line inputs and a stereo pair, each with two-band EQ and effect sends, but bear in mind that this is an eight-track, so you'll be using all these channels for mixing tape tracks. Two stereo returns, so one could be used to bring in virtual tracks, plus a stereo tape input that can only feed the monitors. Multiple memories with auto drop-in/out, and optional £39 remote control.

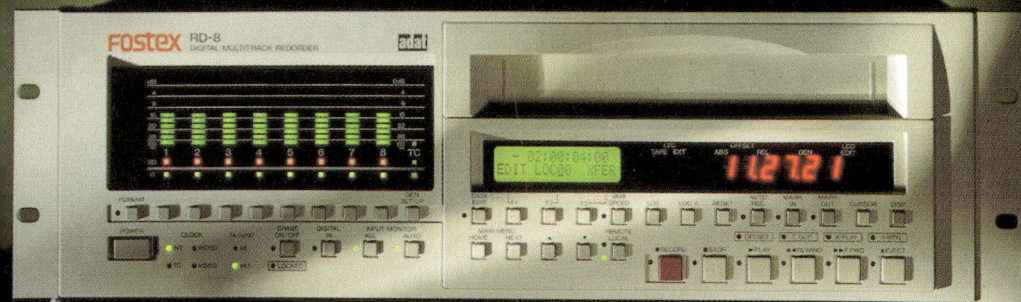

WHY PAY MORE FOR A FOSTEX ADAT?

NOT all digital 8-track recorders are created equal. Our decision to opt for the ADAT format was based on ruggedness, reliability and practicality.

And of course anything with 9 pin serial control will interface with the Fostex RD-8 without the need for additional cards or boxes.

A chase/lock synchroniser with offset is built in as standard, along with an onboard timecode reader/generator.

And when we say 8 tracks, we mean 8 recording tracks. The

timecode is entirely separate.

The RD-8 will also interface directly to any program running Midi Machine Code which means it will fit into your system straight out of the box.

Pick up the 'phone to Fostex and find out more.

We'd be surprised if you didn't get a good connection.

FOSTEX
NOW EVERYTHING CONNECTS

FOSTEX (UK) Ltd. Jackson Way, Great Western Industrial Park, Southall, Middlesex UB2 4SA Great Britain. Tel. 081 893 5111

MICROPHONES

AKG D112: popular and distinctive moving-coil cardioid mike

The sheer variety of microphones on the market today can make choosing a bewildering process – in this chapter we'll look at the main types in general use, and turn the spotlight on a few of the most popular models.

MOVING-COIL, CONDENSER & ELECTRET

These three terms describe how a microphone turns sound into electricity. **Moving-coil** (also called dynamic) is the simplest, and if you take an moving-coil mike to pieces, you'll find that it's almost identical to the 'dome' treble units in moving-coil speakers. A lightweight dome (called the diaphragm) is attached to a coil of wire, and this coil is suspended in a magnetic field; when sound hits the dome, it and the coil move backward and

65

forward, and the movement of the coil in the magnetic field generates electricity. The great attractions of moving-coil mikes are that they're relatively inexpensive to make and (by microphone standards) physically robust. This makes them the obvious choice for stage work.

A **condenser** mike (condenser being the old electrical term for a capacitor) is rather more complicated, but again we start with a lightweight diaphragm, this time suspended a microscopic distance from a metal 'backing plate'. Such an arrangement doesn't generate electricity by itself, but the diaphragm and backing plate together form an electrical component known as a 'capacitor', and if we apply a voltage (called the 'polarising' voltage) across the two, we get an output that varies according to the spacing between them. This output isn't directly of much use, because it's at a very high impedance (see *A Quick Tour*), which would limit us to impractically short cable runs, so we use the polarising voltage to operate a small amplifier inside the mike, which converts the output to low impedance. The polarising voltage is usually 48V, and this is normally supplied by the mixer, using an arrangement called 'phantom power', where the juice uses the same cables that carry the mike's output to the mixer.

Condenser mikes are expensive to make, and relatively fragile, but in many applications they deliver better sound quality than moving-coils, simply because the diaphragm is far lighter than a dome-plus-coil, which in turn allows the treble response to be both more extended and more even, and also enables the mike to capture more of the subtle nuances in a sound. The current buzzword in condensers is 'large-diaphragm', a feature associated with 'warmth', particularly on vocals.

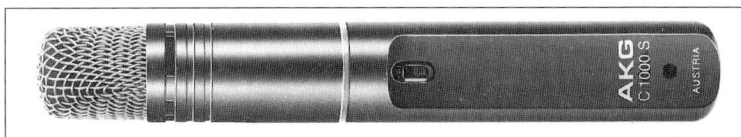

AKGC1000S: most popular electret mike in the £200-300 price bracket

An **electret** mike is very similar to a condenser, except that the diaphragm is made of a metal and plastic mixture that has a polarising voltage 'built in'. We still need a power source though, because we require an impedance-converting amplifier. In cheapish electrets this power is supplied by a battery (sometimes 9V, more often 1.5V), while more expensive jobs offer the choice of battery or phantom power. Using batteries is fine for normal recording, but not really recommended for live use, because Sod's Law says the battery will die in the middle of a gig. Electret mikes have been around for 20-odd years now, but in the early days they acquired a poor reputation – problems included background hiss, distorted treble, and an inability to cope with high sound levels. These nasties are still present in most budget electrets, but there are also some excellent models, usually recognisable by their three-figure price tags.

OMNI-DIRECTIONAL, CARDIOID, HYPER-CARDIOID & FIGURE-OF-EIGHT

Every microphone has what's called a 'pick-up pattern', which describes the mike's sensitivity to sounds coming from different directions. The simplest type is an omni-directional, which is equally sensitive all round. This is useful if you want to mike a group of instruments with just a single microphone, or if you want to capture room reverb along with the 'direct' sound. These situations are quite common with large-scale pro recordings, but rare in semi-pro work. Also, and very importantly, many musos need their mikes to do double duty in live gigs as well as recording, and an omni will easily pick up sound from the PA, which leads to feedback/howlround.

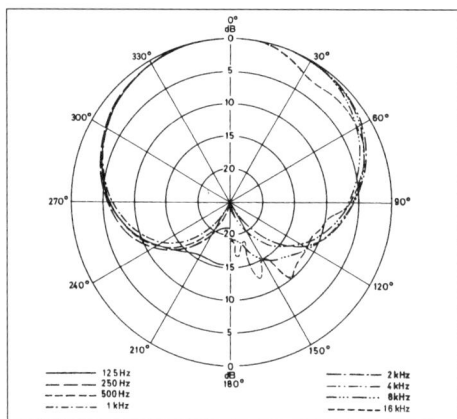

Left: cardioid pick-up pattern; right: business end of the legendary Shure SM58 cardioid

A **cardioid** mike (also called **uni-directional**) has a heart-shaped pickup pattern and is most sensitive to sounds coming from directly in front, with reduced sensitivity at the sides, and almost complete rejection of sounds from the rear. This makes it highly practical for both recording and live work, aspects that are reflected in the fact that cardioids account for about 90 percent of mike sales.

With a name like **hyper-cardioid**, you might think that such a mike is like a cardioid, only even more directional, but this turns out to be only half true. A hyper-cardioid does indeed offer more discrimination between front and side sound sources, but it is actually more sensitive than a cardioid to sounds coming from behind. The rejection of sounds at the sides can help avoid feedback (though this will actually depend on the stage layout), and makes it useful for jobs like close-miking on a drum kit, while some people prefer the results on even relatively simple stuff, like miking a guitar cab.

Both cardioids and hyper-cardioids possess one important peculiarity: what's called the 'proximity effect'. Simply, this means that a mike's frequency response varies according to its distance from the sound source – as the mike and instrument get closer, bass frequencies are boosted. In moderation, this can be quite acceptable and even desirable, adding a degree of 'warmth' to voices for example. But when you get as close as, say, six inches, the effect can become far too strong, and you may well need to use bass cut on the EQ.

The final pick-up pattern we need to consider is the **figure-of-eight**, which provides high sensitivity to both front and rear sounds, but almost total rejection of sounds coming from the sides.

Some condenser mikes (but not electrets) provide switchable pickup patterns, and this is a very useful feature, since you can easily experiment and pick the sound that suits your taste. You may also find switchable bass-cut filters, and a 'pad' to prevent overload at high levels.

VOCAL, INSTRUMENT AND GENERAL-PURPOSE MIKES

Although many microphones can justifiably claim to be good all-rounders, there are lots that acquire a reputation as being particularly suited to certain jobs. In the particular case of moving-coils, this has gone so far that there are two basic types: vocal and instrument. A moving-coil designed for vocals will have reduced output at bass frequencies, which could otherwise tend to be exaggerated and 'muddy', especially with the close-miking proximity effect, and there will also be a peak in the upper-midrange/low-treble, which helps increase clarity and 'presence'. By contrast, an instrument mike will have a much flatter overall response, making it more neutral. This vocal/instrument distinction is all very well in theory, but it's by no means a hard-and-fast rule – you might quite reasonably want to use a vocal type for miking, say, a guitar cab. And to make matters even more complicated, there are many mikes that claim to be general-purpose, which in principle means that they have a response halfway between vocal and instrument types. Personally, I wouldn't bother over-much about any of this – if a mike sounds right on the job(s) you want it for, then right is what it is...

CLIP-ON MIKES

The basic idea of a clip-on microphone is highly attractive – it's physically small, and because it attaches directly to the instrument it's miking, you save on the expense and clutter of a mike stand, and simplify the whole process of miking up. These factors make clip-ons especially appealing for use on drum kits, but though some drummers swear by them, I have to say that I don't generally like the results (and I'm not alone – if clip-ons are a universal solution, how come most pro studios prefer using ordinary mikes?). The basic problem is that, despite their undeniable convenience, clip-ons are essentially very inflexible – they attach to the edge of a drum, so the 'edge-sound' is all you can get, and this will often give a tone very different from that obtained by miking from a few inches above, and angling towards the centre of the drum.

STEREO MIKES

There are lots of stereo microphones available, but few will hold much appeal to semi-pro recordists – the type I think relevant here is what's called an **MS** mike. MS stands for 'middle and side', though 'mono and stereo' might be as good a name, since an MS mike's stereo output provides total compatibility with mono. The 'middle and side' bit refers to the two microphone elements inside the housing: the 'middle' element provides the middle or centre of the stereo soundstage, while the 'side' element is a figure-of-eight type, covering both left and right. MS mikes have gained in popularity over the past few years, not so much for studio recording, but for convenient location work, particularly when 'sample-grabbing' with a portable DAT.

MICROPHONE MODELS

There are so many mikes on the market, particularly in the £80-200 range, that I don't think anyone could claim to have tried them all. What I've done is to pick some of the most popular models and, since we're talking popularity, one mike immediately stands out from the crowd: the **Shure SM58**. This cardioid moving-coil vocal model has been around for something like 35 years, and though you might think this would mean that it's totally outdated, it actually remains fully competitive (£150 list price). Tough as old boots, the 58 is an obvious choice for combined recording and live use, and a special attraction over its many lookalike competitors is simply that everybody's heard of it, which makes it far easier to sell secondhand if ever you move upmarket. But though the 58 is a fine mike for the price, it isn't necessarily your best choice – you might find an alternative that is better suited to your voice. It's probably unfair to pick just one model from the vast array of competitors, but I'm going to do it anyway, and nominate the **Beyer M300**. I find that this gives a slightly warmer sound than the 58, yet at the same time delivers more detail, and has the advantage of being 20 quid cheaper.

Musos who can't stretch to this kind of money will, sadly, have to accept that cheaper mikes just don't sound as good (with just one rather special/weird exception we'll consider later). At the £50 mark, the **Shure Prologue 14** provides decent overall results, but with a definite loss of detail, while I've also heard favourable reports on the £65 **AKG D80**.

Moving up from SM58 territory, three moving-coil cardioids enjoy particular success: the **AKG D112** (£205), **Beyer M201** (£260), and **Sennheiser MD421** (£330). The D112 (known as 'the egg', on account of its unusual shape) is widely used for bass drum miking, but some people like it for all sorts of things, including bass guitar and even vocals, while both the Beyer and Sennheiser offerings are excellent general-purpose workhorses.

The £200-300 price range also opens the door on 'serious' electret mikes, of which by far the most popular is the **AKG C1000S** (£270). This can use battery or phantom power, and comes with a slip-on adaptor to convert from cardioid to hyper. It can do a very credible job on vocals, but its prime role is as a versatile instrument mike.

And so we come to 'true' condenser models, the prices of most of which are likely to daunt all but the keenest musos. The good news here is the arrival of the **Oktava** brand from Russia, with the cardioid **MK219** at £311, and the cardioid/hyper/omni **MK012** at £352. By condenser standards, these prices are almost laughably cheap, and the sound quality is fine. But paying more can provide better results still – models to consider include the **Audio-Technica AT4033** (£590), **AKG C3000** (currently £530, but apparently about to be reduced) and **C414** (£980), and the **Neumann TLM 193** (£960). Both of the AKGs have switchable pick-up patterns, and though all the above models carry seriously heavyweight price tags, they also deliver seriously heavyweight quality.

And now, from the sublime to... the **Tandy PZM**. Selling for just £35, it would be easy to dismiss this as a toy. But you'd be making a big mistake. PZM stands for **pressure-zone** microphone, also known as a **boundary** mike, and while we don't need to bother about the theory behind these names, what's important is that, for many recording purposes, the PZM is simply *the* budget mike. It's an electret (which at this price is usually Bad News), and unlike every other mike I've mentioned, it has an unbalanced output (see *A Quick Tour*). One look at it tells you this is no ordinary mike, and instead of using it on a conventional mike stand, you mount it on a floor, wall, or any large flat surface (which makes it even cheaper than it seems, because you don't need a stand). Weirder still, its pick-up pattern doesn't fit any of the types we've looked at – it's **hemispherical**, which means it's equally sensitive to all sounds coming from anywhere in front of the surface it's mounted on.

When you put all these aspects together, you get a mike that's hopeless for stage use (though quite effective for recording the overall sound at a gig). But for home recording work, it can produce results that simply defy belief. Many times it delivers sound quality, for example on vocals and acoustic guitar, that can easily be passed off as coming from a mike at five or more times the price. You'll find some thoughts on the practical aspects of using the PZM in *Miking Up*, and if you can cope with these, the PZM is, to underline what I said above, simply the best budget recording mike ever. Get it, or regret it.

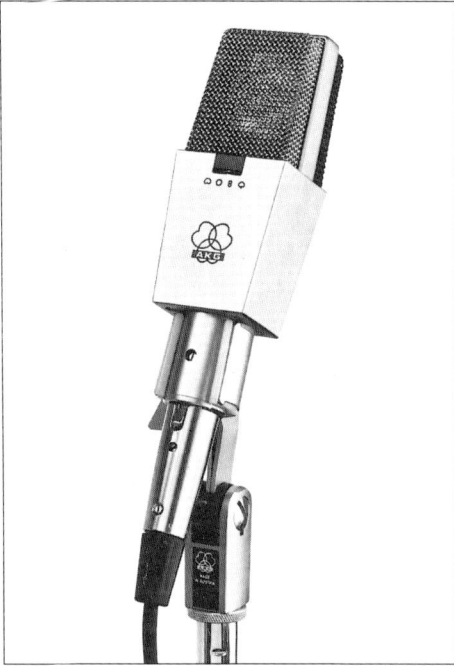

Some recommended models. Above left: AKGC414; above right: Audio-Technica AT-4033.
Below left: Neumann TLM193; below right: Sennheiser MD421; bottom right: Tandy PZM

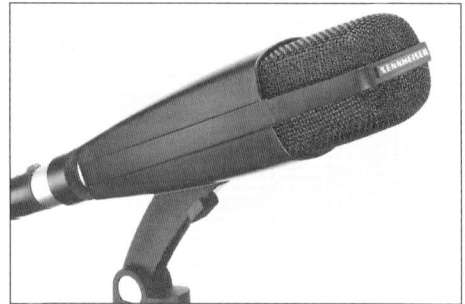

EFFECTS

Many musos, particularly guitarists, will already be familiar with lots of effects, and there's absolutely no reason why guitar-style goodies like chorus, flanging, phasing and even 'overdrive' can't be used in general recording work, not only with keyboards, but also with vocals and less common instruments (you ain't lived 'til you've heard a chorused, flanged harmonica...). We'll first take a look at the basic effects that figure in most commercial recordings, and then mention a few popular models.

The ART of rackmounting effects. The company's FXR unit is a recommended budget buy

EQ

We've already examined most types of EQ under *Mixer Features* – the one I want to consider here is graphic equalisation. Graphics have all but replaced bass 'n' treble controls on 'midi' hi-fi systems, but though there's no

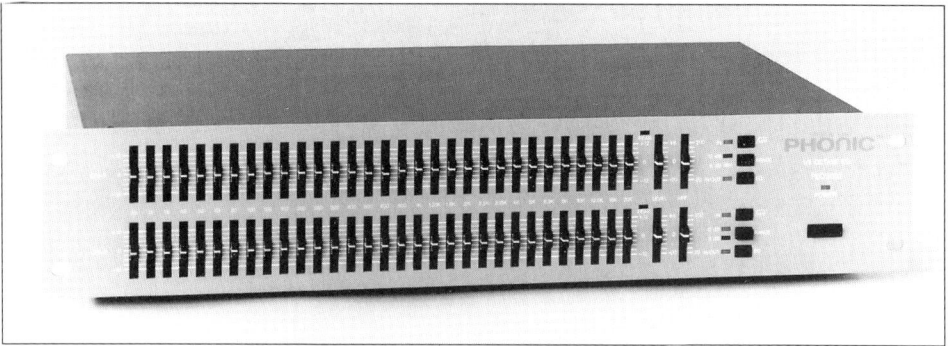

Among budget graphics, this 31-band stereo Phonic PEQ3600 gets favourable reports

doubt they look good in the techno-cred stakes, their usefulness in recording depends very much on the number of 'bands'. A five-band (as fitted to some multi-track cassette recorders) is better than nothing, but ten-band is far more flexible. And if you're serious, you really want a 31-band graphic (also called a one-third octave EQ, because each band's centre frequency is about a third of an octave higher or lower than the next). Such a graphic can be a very useful tool, but there are two points: it can take a lot longer to set up than, say, a parametric, and quite a few graphics have some pretty undesirable effects on the sound quality of signals passing through them.

A common application for graphics is in monitoring, where they're supposed to correct for speaker and, particularly, room pecularities. I can't actually go so far as to say that they're useless for this, but there are an awful lot of monitoring problems that they very definitely can't do anything to rectify, and I certainly wouldn't recommend anyone to buy a graphic for this purpose without trying it first.

ECHO AND REVERB

Echo is a simple concept – you shout into a canyon, the sound travels until it hits the canyon wall, where some of the energy is absorbed, but most is reflected, so it bounces back, and eventually reaches your ears as a distinct echo. Echo can be very effective (sorry) in music production, the main practical point being that in order for it to work properly, you need to be able to fine-tune the delay time exactly to match the tempo/BPM of the music.

The first step up from this basic idea is to feed some of the echo back into the processor, so you get another, fainter, echo a little later, and then another, and so on (in canyon terms, it's like the sound bouncing back and forth between the walls). The next development is what's called 'multi-tapped' echo, which is primarily a performance-type effect, originally for guitar, though it could be used with keyboards or even vocals. Instead of just a single echo, or even multiple echoes with a fixed time between them, you get several

Yamaha REV5: one of the company's high specification dedicated digital reverberators

separate echoes at different times. These in turn can be fed back to produce further echoes, and you may also be able to control where all these echoes appear on the stereo soundstage.

Reverb is basically a more complex version of multi-tapped echo, except that in this case the echoes are so many, and so close together, that we don't hear them as separate echoes, but rather as what might be called an overall 'after-glow'. Two obvious examples of this are a concert hall and a bathroom, though we'd expect the results from each to be very different. This difference is caused by several factors, most notably the size and shape of the room, the surfaces of the walls, floor and ceiling, and where in the room you and the sound source are positioned. All of these are the things you're effectively controlling when you select a particular program on a reverb unit. Some reverbs offer literally hundreds of alternatives, while others provide just a few, but with the facility to 'edit' or customise them to taste.

DYNAMICS PROCESSORS: LIMITERS, COMPRESSORS, NOISE GATES, EXPANDERS, DYNAMIC NOISE LIMITERS

You may think I'm going for an entry in the *Guinness Book of Records* under 'longest sub-heading in history', but all of these items belong together, because they're all about modifying the 'natural' dynamics of your music.

A **limiter** is a fairly crude device, though virtually vital in many PA applications, so we'll look at it briefly first, because it opens the way to more sophisticated dynamics processors. It doesn't really matter whether we're talking about PA or recording – as you increase the signal level there comes a point above which the system stops producing more volume, and simply produces more distortion. This kind of overload distortion is audibly very unpleasant, and a limiter simply stops signals from reaching the critical level.

74

Unfortunately, there are limits (ho, ho) to what a limiter can achieve. But since it can often make a PA sound like it's got twice the wattage it actually has, spending £250 on such a device can seem like a real bargain compared with increasing your PA power from, say, 500 to 1000watts (plus, it can protect your speakers against getting blown-up).

A **compressor** is much more useful in recording work, and as the name suggests, it compresses or reduces the dynamic range. The result of this is to make your music sound louder without actually increasing its peak level, and it's a well-known fact that, in general terms, louder sounds better. About 99 percent of commercial music uses compression to some extent, and the effect is used very heavily both in TV commercials and radio broadcasts (listen to a fade-out when a station is playing a track off vinyl, and you'll hear the surface noise come up dramatically due to the compression).

A **noise gate** is basically a muting device, the term gate being used because it can either be open, letting the signal through, or closed, which mutes the signal. Apart from the obvious application of killing 'dead-air' on an

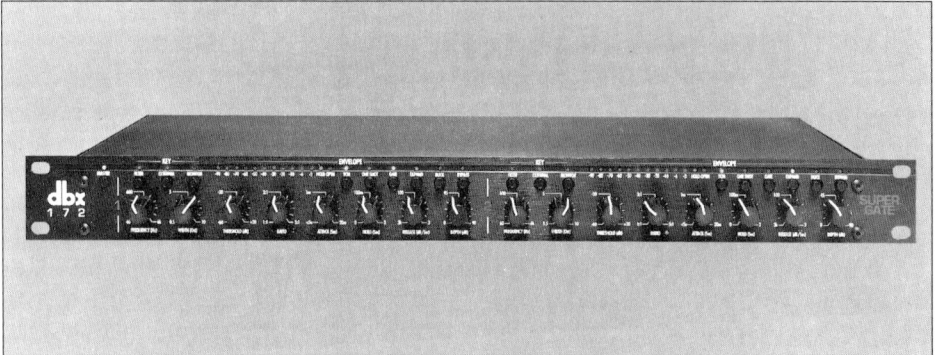

The dbx 172 Super Gate offers sophisticated stereo noise gate facilities

unwanted channel or track, its main use is to rhythmically 'tighten' sounds in a mix, often on bass guitar and snare drum.

An **expander** is a more versatile device and, as you might guess, it acts as the opposite of a compressor, effectively increasing dynamic range. **Dynamic noise limiters** are also more subtle versions of a noise gate – they don't actually go as far as opening and closing, but instead 'monitor' the frequency makeup of the signal, and filter out the treble when the signal level at high frequencies is low enough to make hiss audible. These devices need fine-tuning to work effectively, but they can then be very useful at the end of an effects chain.

Extra features to look for on dynamics processors include what's called 'side-chain access', which can, for example, enable you to use a compressor as a 'de-esser' to reduce vocal sibilance, and a 'key' or 'trigger' input on noise gates, which allows you to use one sound (like a bass drum) to 'trigger' another (like a super-deep bass synth).

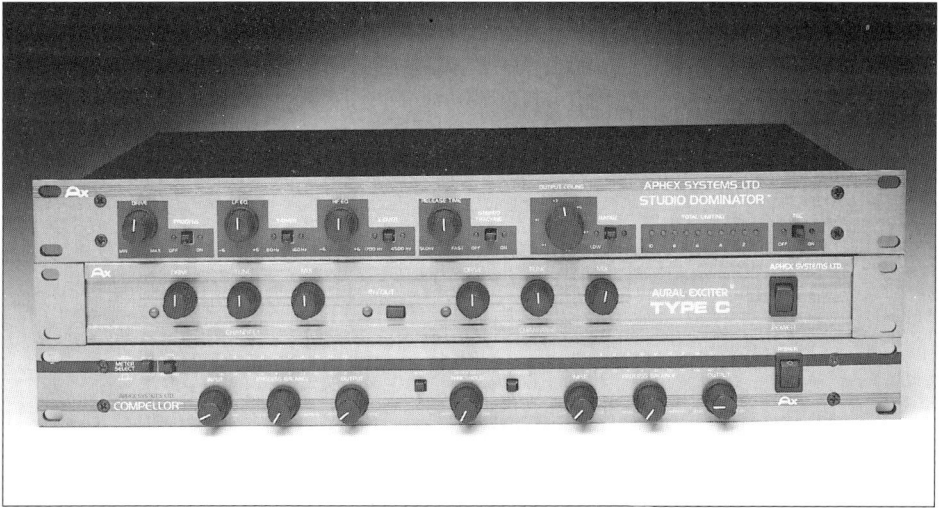

Trio of Aphex units including the legendary Aural Exciter – the original enhancer

ENHANCERS

The original enhancers were produced by Aphex and called Aural Exciters – Aphex held a trademark on the term exciter, so everybody else had to find a different name for their equivalents, hence the term enhancer.

As is often the case, the basic idea is quite simple, but the results can be, to say the least, highly attention-grabbing. The principle starts from the simple fact that, if you want to make something stand out in a mix, you make it louder. Trouble is, this upsets the mix balance. The enhancer gets around this by working on the treble harmonics in a signal which, though usually low in level, nevertheless affect our perception of the overall sound.

But it is not a question of simply boosting the treble – even a basic enhancer is much more refined than that. What it does is to take the existing treble and use it to generate more treble, with the new stuff being an octave higher than the original. Applied in large doses, this adds obvious 'sparkle', even to the point of being annoying, but in more moderate use, most listeners don't notice any direct effect, they simply find the effected signal more 'attractive' and interesting. Some enhancers do other things as well, such as what's called 'pulse-width manipulation', but all you really need to know is that, whatever the tech-talk, the objective is to make a signal stand out by manipulating the treble.

A more recent application of this concept works at the *bass* end of things. As with treble enhancers, there's quite a variety of tricks that can be used (such as goodies like 'phase-shifting'), but the most common is simply to use the existing bass to generate a new component that is an octave lower in pitch. Unlike treble enhancement, this has a very definite effect on signal levels and perceived loudness, adding both 'power' and 'depth' to the bass.

MULTI-EFFECT UNITS

Ten years ago, an effect processor that could produce more than one type of effect was a rarity – today it's the norm. Part of the reason for this is the increasing power and decreasing price of digital electronics, but it's also been happening with effects that are still, usually, analogue – such as dynamics processors. In the case of dynamics units, there's a lot to be said for a multi-effect processor, because it should mean that the manufacturer has, for example, designed his noise gate and expander to complement the action of his compressor. With digital systems, you need to consider how many of the various effects are available at the same time, and how much flexibility you've got in choosing the order/sequence in which the effects operate. A potentially important point is that, though you may be able to have several effects simultaneously, you can't usually apply them to separate signals, so you can't, for example, have echo on one track and reverb on another. Also, if you want to be able to use an effect on an overall mix, you'll not surprisingly need a stereo (ie two-channel) processor – bear in mind that while most units have stereo *outputs*, many at the budget end of things have only one (mono) *input*.

Alesis Quadraverb GT: one of many good buys among the multi-effects genre

SELECTED MODELS

GRAPHIC EQ
At the budget end I've heard favourable reports on **Phonic** models, at £165 for a 31-band, and £269 for a dual 31-band; also the **Alesis MEQ 230** (dual 30-band) at £259. As with most effects, there are many, many mid-price models, so rather than chop down a small rainforest to print all the details, I'll pick just two: the catchily-named **Yamaha GQ1031BII** (£299 31-band), and its dual-channel brother, the **Q2031A** (£549).

ECHO AND REVERB
Most such units also provide a variety of 'guitar-style' effects, such as phasing, flanging and chorus. **ART** get a prize for their budget .**FXR**, with 250 presets for £199, simply because it can work in stereo or as two separate mono processors, which is unusual at this kind of price. At the same price there's

the highly-competent **Alesis Microverb III**, while £389 buys you the **Lexicon ALEX**, which may have only 16 programs but gives you a taste of why some super-pro studios pay up to ten grand for Lexicon's big reverbs.

DYNAMICS

Drawmer and **dbx** are both well-known for their professional dynamics processors, and both now have models aimed at the semi-pro user. **Drawmer** offer the **LX20** dual-channel compressor/expander (otherwise known as a 'compander') at £229, while **dbx** have the **266** dual channel compressor/gate at £329. **Behringer** have several models, notably including the £236 dual-channel **Autocom** compressor/limiter, and the £342 dual-channel **Composer** compressor/limiter/expander (all Behringer kit carries a highly-credible five-year guarantee).

ENHANCERS

Steal of the year here has to be the dual-channel **Behringer Dualfex II**, which combines basic treble and bass enhancement for just £149. There's also a more refined version, the **Ultrafex**, at £257. Enhacement originators Aphex have their marvellously-monickered Aural Exciter with Big Bottom listing at £299.

MULTI-EFFECT UNITS

Most of the effect units above are, to a greater or lesser extent, multi-effect processors. But the ones I'm considering here take the idea much further, combining a variety of recording effects with some, or even a lot of, guitar-style stuff – remember what I said at the beginning of this chapter about many guitar effects being potential useful with other instruments.

There's the **Alesis Quadraverb+** at £399 and **Quadraverb GT** at £359 and **Quadraverb 2** at £899; the **Yamaha EMP700** (£519) and highly-regarded **SPX990** (£799), plus what dealer friends tell me is current 'flavour-of-the-month' with consumers, the **Sony HR-MP5** at £499, along with its more guitar-orientated brother, the **HR-GP5**. Other 'take seriously' models include the **Boss SE-70** from Roland at £625, and **Peavey SDR-2020** at £649.

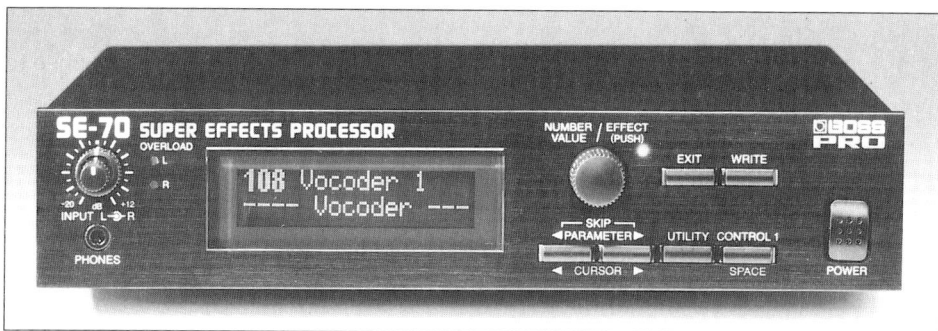

Boss SE-70 from Roland: another multi-effector worthy of serious consideration

MONITORING

A pair of Epos ES14s will cost you £585, but headphones suitable for foldback start at £11

The importance of decent-quality monitoring simply can't be over-emphasised – as I said in *A Quick Tour*, if you can't hear it, you can't fix it or mix it. This is all very well, but when you consider that a typical pro studio will spend £5000+ on its main speakers and amplifiers, it's clear that most of us will have to compromise in a fairly big way.

The worst case is where, having bought the necessary recording gear, you've simply run out of money – so your monitor system is whatever lo/mid/hi-fi you happen to have lying around. In many cases, this will be some sort of variation on the 'midi'/rack theme, and we may as well face up to the fact that almost all of these, no matter how expensive, are pretty appalling in the sound quality stakes. If nothing else (and there's usually plenty else), they're let down by their speakers.

Still, if this is what you're stuck with, the name of the game is making the most of it. And the big trick here is not to mix your productions so they sound as good as possible, but to mix them so they sound wrong in the same ways as commercial recordings – common examples include boomy mid-bass and shrieky treble. If you don't already know what your gear is doing wrong, take some of your favourite material along to a good local hi-fi dealer (check the *Yellow Pages*) and have a listen.

The same principles apply even if your system is 'real' hi-fi – no audio gear is perfect, and it's important to get to know its strengths, weaknesses, and idiosyncracies, along with whatever acoustic effects your room introduces.

If you're in the happy position of being able to spend some dosh on the monitoring department, then you could also be headed for a fair-sized nervous breakdown. There are well over a thousand different speakers and amps on the market; worse, most of these will be superseded within a year or two, so there's seldom time for a product to build up a long-term reputation (in the way of, say, the Shure SM58). The only places you can turn for help are magazine reviews and retailers, but there are problems with both of these. The point about reviews is that they're far more opinion than fact, and even when the opinions are well-informed, they remain subjective. Two reviewers may disagree completely (something about 'one man's meat…'), in much the same way that a Tory and a Labourite can draw very different conclusions from the same facts.

The answer may lie in listening at a shop, but there are pitfalls even here. For a start, you're listening to the demonstration room's acoustics as much as the hi-fi; also, in many cases, using the dealer's choice of other hardware. But, most importantly, you're probably only listening for a relatively short period of time, and on a relatively small selection of music. This is Not Good. Comparisons with cars and, of all things, perfumes, spring to mind – you test-drive a car, and you notice all sorts of things: headroom, legroom, steering lightness, and much more. But even then, there will be many more items that you only begin to notice when you've actually had the car for several weeks. The perfume comparison is relevant because a smell, or a sound, that is initially exciting can easily become tiring with longer exposure; likewise, something that doesn't hit you over the head to begin with may well become more persuasive with time. Many hi-fi dealers recognise these limitations, and offer home trials – this is an excellent idea, but the retailers who offer this facility often tend to be the ones who expect you to pay full retail price for the privilege.

So far, I've been treating hi-fi and monitoring as pretty much one and the same thing, but one major potential difference is the ability of serious monitoring gear to play seriously loud, something that is quite beyond almost all budget and mid-price hi-fi. Really high volumes are only strictly necessary when laying down tracks, to ensure that you've got a 'clean' signal – no hum, hiss, crackles, distortion, etc, and this is something that can easily be checked using headphones. Many engineers and producers actually do their 'mix' monitoring on speakers that have more in common with domestic hi-fi, and these are referred to as 'mini-monitors', as distinct from the monstrously large and loud 'main' monitors.

Another aspect of the hi-fi/monitoring business is the use of the word

Recommended speakers: £150 Mission 760iSE (left); Monitor Audio MA202 (right) at £400

'monitor' itself. Once again, the comparison is with cars – you can stick the label GT on any old piece of junk, but it doesn't necessarily mean a thing (a secondhand car dealer once told me that a Grand Tourer was any car with a spare tyre). Thus it is with the label 'monitor', which is typically used on ultra-budget gear. Making matters more complicated, there are quite a few speakers, usually sold through music rather than hi-fi shops, that claim to have monitoring, as distinct from hi-fi, qualities, but at the same sort of prices as midrange hi-fi. I've listened to several such, and though generalisations are dangerous, I've found them no better and no worse than similarly-priced hi-fi speakers.

What we've got so far is that, for most of us, our main monitors will be what a pro studio would call its minis. But we still need our own version of mini-monitors, to provide a guide to how the mix will sound on really cheap gear. Almost anything will do for this, and the most practical item is a stereo radio-cassette with line inputs, the main point being that, as with all monitoring, you need to get to know its 'sound'.

Something that often causes confusion is the term 'near-field'. This simply means a speaker that is designed to give its best results when used quite close to the listening position (typically, about four feet away). The attractions of near-field monitoring are that you get loud sounds without needing high power (less risk of annoying family/neighbours), and that you slightly reduce the extent to which room acoustics will 'colour' the sound. Not all speakers are suitable for this kind of work though, because the output from their bass/mid and treble drive units doesn't 'integrate' until you get further away. As with the term monitor, there are several budget speakers with 'near-field' in their names, but in my experience, it doesn't mean a thing.

Note that some speakers are designed for use close to a wall, while others need to be a couple of feet into the room – this is important because, if you use them incorrectly, you either get too little or too much bass.

OK, let's take a look at some specific products (bearing in mind that, as I said about hi-fi reviews, we're talking personal opinions). If you're totally and utterly strapped for cash, I suggest a **Sherwood AI-2210 amplifier** (£60 and 30W a channel), with a pair of **JPW Mini Monitors** (also £60). An extra £20 buys the rather better **JPW Gold Monitors**. The sound is as good as I'm aware you can get for the price, but that said, it's bass-light, 'congested' in the midrange, 'glassy' in the treble, and distinctly limited in loudness. Thought you'd like to know. One reason these items are so cheap is that they're exclusive to the Richer Sounds hi-fi chain – freephone 0500 10 11 12 for a catalogue and store locations.

There are lots of speakers around the £100–120 mark, but in many cases the improvement over the Gold Monitors is marginal, so we'll move on up to £150, where there is one speaker that I, and many reviewers, regard as a real winner: the **Mission 760iSE**. You could use this with the budget Sherwood, but my own recommendation is the next model up the Sherwood ladder, the £100 50W **AI-1110**, which I find easily matches most amps at twice the price for both power and sound quality.

In the £200-300 speaker range I haven't, to my surprise, found a model that really stands out from the crowd – the £250 **Royd Minstrel** has many fine qualities, but doesn't like high volumes or heavy bass, while the identically-priced **Monitor Audio MA-201** has collected some excellent write-ups, but for my taste is rather too bright. This is strange, because it uses exactly the same drivers as the next model I'm going to recommend, the £400 **Monitor Audio MA-202**. This gives you a big box for your bucks, and delivers impressively deep and powerful bass. The 202 is a floor-stander, which means that the drive units are only at the right height when you sit in an easy chair – if you're working at a mixer, you'll probably need 12- or 18-inch stands, and these could add £70 to the bill.

If you can afford still more, check out the £585 **Epos ES14**. This doesn't have quite the immediate low-end 'clout' of the 202, but is a far more refined overall performer. Many 'experts' will tell you that the ES14 needs a very expensive amplifier (like £1500-worth), but I find it works a treat with the £100 Sherwood. I'm not saying you can't get a better amp if you spend more; simply that, in my opinion, you'd do better to spend £700 this way, rather than the more obvious approach of £350 speakers with a £350 amp.

And finally, headphones... There are two basic types: open- and closed-back. Open-backs generally give better sound quality, but their construction means that sound leaks out, and this 'spill' will be picked up by nearby mikes. Sound quality isn't usually a big issue for foldback, and Argos do a closed-back **Sony** for just £11. At the other extreme, you could go for the 'standard' pro model, the **Beyer DT-100**, a snip (?) at £120.

STEREO RECORDERS

Unless money is no object, DAT is really the only sensible choice for stereo mastering

You may be buying a recorder to mix your multi-track masters to stereo, or you may be recording 'live' to stereo, as do the increasing number of muso-recordists working with virtual tracks. Either way, you want the maximum sound per pound from your stereo deck.

There are really just three format options: Compact Cassette, DAT and analogue open-reel. I've listed them in this order, simply because it's how your choices open up as the price rises. The sound quality argument isn't quite so straightforward, because, for example, a really good cassette can beat a bad DAT in many respects. You'll notice I haven't mentioned DCC (Digital Compact Cassette) or MiniDisc – first-generation products for both these media had limitations, and though the latest gear is apparently much better, there really isn't any certainty that either format will still be well-supported in, say, ten years' time (anyone remember Sony Elcaset?).

COMPACT CASSETTE

Choosing a budget cassette deck used to be easy – just about every reviewer in town waxed lyrical about the £120 **Aiwa AD-F410**, and it had been on the market long enough to build an enviable reputation. But now it's being replaced by the identically-priced **AD-F450**, and it's too early yet to say whether Aiwa have managed to keep the 410's sound quality (not something you can take for granted in hi-fi). With Dolby B, C, HX Pro and music search, its only obvious let-down is the rudimentary metering.

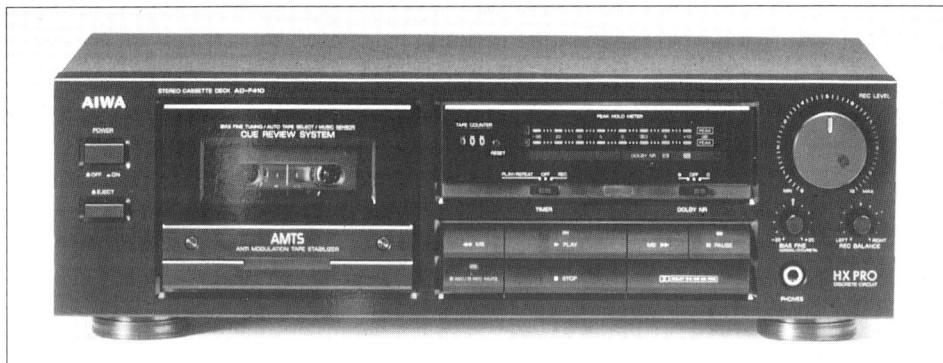

Aiwa AD-F410: top-rated budget cassette deck, only recently superseded by the AD-F450

Amazingly, there are no acknowledged clear winners between here and almost double the price, and while many of the contenders have better features than the budget Aiwa, their sound quality is often no better. At £200 there's the **Pioneer CT-S 430S**, currently the cheapest Dolby S deck on the UK market, but again, it's a new model, so performance is still an unknown quantity. And at £230, it's **Aiwa** time again, with the recently-introduced **AD-F850**, replacing the long-established and well-rated **AD-F810**. Though there's no Dolby S, your money gets you three heads (allowing off-tape monitoring), and a dual-capstan drive. First reports say that it's as good as the old 810, so it looks like a safe bet.

At the £300 mark three models compete head-on: the **Aiwa AD-F950**, **Pioneer CT-S 630S**, and **Sony TC-K 611S**. All three offer similar features (most notably Dolby S and three heads), but the Pioneer and Sony also have auto tape set-up, which is a lot more convenient than fiddling with the Aiwa's manual set-up. The Sony also has the advantage of having been around long enough to pick up a *What Hi-fi* magazine award.

Bridging the gap between here and DAT territory is the legendary **Nakamichi** range, whose cheapest model, the **DR-3**, lists at £400. No Dolby S here, and only a simple single-capstan, two-head design. But one listen tells you why Nakamichi can get away with their prices – the sound quality is in a different league from cheaper machines. Look inside, and you'll find far better build quality too, which generally translates into a longer working life (a friend of mine has a 12-year-old Nakamichi still in daily use).

There are plenty of more expensive cassette decks, but at just about any price you name, you'll find there's a Nakamichi to take the honours. More realistically though, once your budget gets much above £400, it's time to think about...

DIGITAL AUDIO TAPE

DAT was the first serious attempt to bring CD-digital quality to a user-recordable format. As a mass-consumer medium, it bombed almost unnoticed, but in the professional world it is now by far the dominant stereo mastering format.

Given that DAT machines start from under £600, this is pretty important, but though even the cheapest DAT machines deliver the format's two basic performance points of no audible hiss or wow/flutter, they don't always sound terribly good (he said politely). Early models (rather like early CD players) tended to harshness, but my main complaint about the current budget DATs I've auditioned is a 'blandness' that both flattens and deadens the sound. Also, it must be said that budget DAT does not enjoy much of a reputation for reliability or even robustness. I recently had some wholly unamusing experiences with two samples of a DAT machine that chewed tape whenever another tape deck (maybe ten pounds in weight) was placed on top of them.

A potentially major point that separates domestic DATs from pro machines is the appalling and pointless SCMS (acronym for Serial Copy Management System – appropriately pronounced 'scums'). SCMS is appalling because it stops you doing digital copies from one DAT to another (you can still make copies through the analogue outs-to-ins, but the extra stages and conversions tend to degrade sound quality). It's pointless because, though supposedly built into the DAT format at the insistence of record company paranoids terrified at the prospect of organised digital piracy, even record industry people might have been able to comprehend that SCMS wouldn't deter a professional pirate for more than five minutes.

Still, SCMS is what you'll get on virtually all domestic DATs. Only on machines costing £1,000 or more is it either ignored completely or made a switchable option. Some buyers want digital-digital copying enough to pay the extra for SCMS-free DATs; on the other hand, a good many thousand UK recordists have happily bought SCMS-equipped decks. Another option is to buy a SCMS deck, then pay around £150 extra for a 'SCMS-stripper', which is a little black box that removes the offending digital code. Some suppliers will now sell you a DAT with the stripper added internally, which works out slightly cheaper.

The cheapest current DAT is the **Sony TCD-D7** portable at £550. This must be a highly attractive proposition if you want to combine mixdown

At £800, the choice is between this Aiwa XDS-1100 DAT machine or Sony's DTC-60ES

recording with location 'sample-grabbing', but it might be unreasonable to expect a budget portable to handle a really heavy workload without problems, and you'd probably get frustrated with the tiny buttons and meters.

At £800 you have the choice of the **Aiwa XDS-1100** (distributed by HHB) or the **Sony DTC-60ES**. The Sony features a clever little number called SBM (Super Bit Mapping), which improves dynamic range by shifting noise from the midrange, where our ears are particularly sensitive, to the high treble region. I've auditioned SBM and, yes, it works, but the effect is mighty subtle under most circumstances. The Sony's layout, with well-sized and positioned controls, is rather more user-friendly than the fiddly layout on the Aiwa, but there's currently something of a question-mark over Sony's attitude to in-guarantee service.

This has been a 'running sore' in the letters pages of recording magazines for almost a year now, with complaints alleging that Sony have refused free guarantee service on faulty DATs, on the grounds that the machines had suffered more wear than Sony felt was reasonable. This is real 'can of worms' stuff, with Sony's legal department saying that the law recognises the 'common-sense' point that a product, though purportedly guaranteed for, say, a year, cannot be expected to be guaranteed if it is actually used more than a certain amount during the year. The Catch 22 is that Sony can't/won't say exactly how much that 'certain amount' of use is (they say every case is considered individually), but for me the bottom-line is: only buy Sony from a dealer who will write 'One-year unlimited-use guarantee provided by XYZ Retailer Ltd' on the receipt, since this makes the *retailer* legally responsible regardless of Sony's position. This being the case, it helps to choose a retailer you think will still be around 364 days later to sort out any problem...

Moving further up in price, we enter the crossover territory between domestic (SCMS) and professional DAT. **Fostex**, **Otari**, **Panasonic**,

Spending over £1000? Panasonic is one of many names offering professional DAT decks

Pioneer, **Sony** and **Tascam** all feature here, and apart from the wholly unlamented loss of SCMS on some machines, you also have options like timecode and jog/shuttle. Picking just a couple of machines, I find the **Tascam DA-30** offers a good standard of basic features and sound quality for £1350. The high-speed **Pioneer D-07** (£1150) is attractive for its superb sound quality, but like a high-speed multi-track cassette machine, this isn't much use if you want other people with standard-speed machines to be able to play your tapes.

OPEN-REEL

Open-reel analogue recorders start at just under a grand, and though we could easily get into an interesting debate about the sound quality pros and cons relative to DAT, what matters is that the music industry position is that it couldn't give a toss – DAT's adequate, practical and convenient, and DAT's all there is to say (sorry).

If you prefer the analogue 'sound' to the point where you're prepared to shell out for it, then there is a whole hierachy of models by **Tascam**, plus the ever-popular **Revox** series. One aspect to think about: stereo open-reels generally come without noise reduction. A 65-70dB dynamic range is probably par for the course, and entirely adequate for many types of music, but if you fully explore the *ppp* to *fff* range, then hiss could be a problem. Also, come the happy day when somebody wants to stick something you've done on cassette/ vinyl/CD, which would you rather mail them – a 10½in reel or a DAT?

If money's no object, by all means check out analogue, but since money is decidedly relevant to most buyers, my general advice is to get a decent DAT, and spend the dosh you save on, maybe, a better mike, or a second reverb.

ACCESSORIES

MIKE STANDS

The ideal mike stand would combine flexible and effortless adjustment, complete stability, and total acoustic inertness/deadness. Here in the real world, most musos settle for a £40-45 stand with boom arm, and though you might think that such stands would be much of a muchness, it turns out that there are quite a number of aspects to consider.

Starting from the ground up, mike stand bases come in two basic types: three-legged and cast-iron circular. Three-legged stands are generally more stable (particularly with boom arms), and on some models the legs can be folded up for storage and transport – check the mechanism used for this, both for ease of operation and secure locking. Circular-base stands are useful whenever you need a small 'footprint', most obviously when close-miking a drum kit, but also where there's a risk of someone tripping over a stand's legs.

Most columns will have two sections, and the locking mechanism is worth a close look – as with collapsible legs, you're after ease of use and secure locking. Beware of 'pneumatic'/air-suspension stands – these are ideal in their intended stage application, which is to adjust easily for different vocalists, but can be a real nuisance in recording work.

The boom arm will screw on to the top of the column, and it's important that you can do this up really tightly, otherwise the arm will start to unscrew itself every time you turn it anti-clockwise. There will be a lock on the boom arm tilt adjustment, and you'll find two distinct versions: a circular knob or a lever. It may be personal preference (or it may be that I'm a weakling), but I vastly prefer the lever type – it's hard to grip a knob tightly enough to really lock the arm in place. (Many levers tend to rattle; cure this with a good-sized blob of BluTack.) There will be a small knob to lock the arm extension, and this almost always causes problems when you want to use the arm vertically with a heavyish microphone. Heavy mikes can also be troublesome with the arm fully extended horizontally – this is because budget stands usually have a small fixed counterweight; a heavier adjustable counterweight is a definite feature to look for if you're prepared to pay a bit more.

The final component is the mike holder itself – this will normally come with the mike, but it's worth mentioning here that some holders are almost totally useless. The worst case is when you're using an SM58-style mike facing straight down – if you don't push it in far enough, it falls out; if you do, the holder snaps (my favourite replacement holder for this type of mike is the **AKG SA41**, £10.50).

For some home recording purposes, you might consider an alternative to 'traditional' mike stands, in the shape of a 'multi-poise' stand. As the name suggests, this is based on the classic Anglepoise lamp, but with a G-clamp instead of the usual base. I particularly recommend this type of stand for vocals and acoustic guitar, not only because it avoids the clutter of an ordinary stand, but also because it's easier to position.

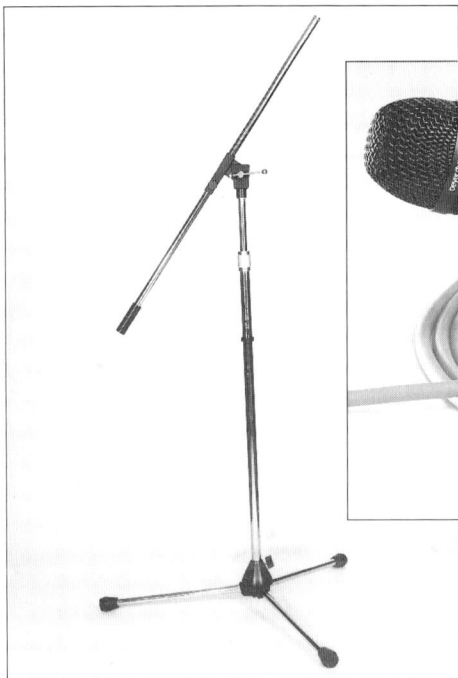

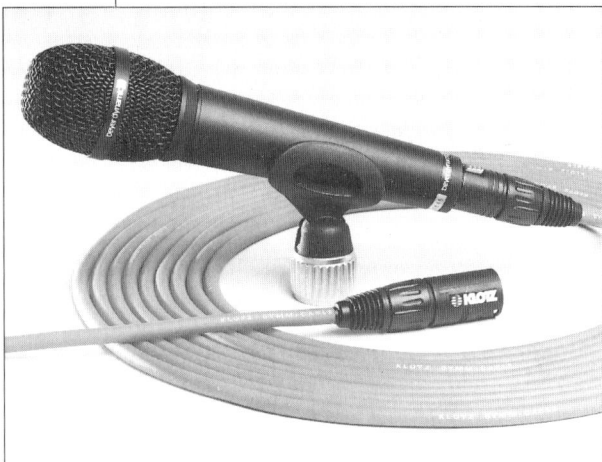

Left: boom stand with tripod base.
Above: the 'Klotz' name is a good enough
guarantee of 'real' cable for semi-pro
recording purposes

CABLES, CONNECTORS AND ADAPTORS

As with mike stands, cables turn out to be a lot more complicated than you might suppose. The two basic points are that all cables have an effect on sound quality, and that cables with fewer (and more benign) effects can get very, very pricey, especially in the quantities needed for many home studios.

At the very bottom end of the market is the kind of rubbish supplied free with hi-fi gear. You can buy a stereo one-metre pair for under a pound, but even a modest monitoring set-up will reveal its sonic limitations when compared with 'real' cable. But what is 'real' cable? Certainly we can forget the kind of stuff serious hi-fi enthusiasts use, because although the sound quality can be utterly superb, the prices can be utterly silly (I'm currently using **Insert Audio** solid silver interconnects, at £64 a half-metre pair, and even this is considered no more than mid-price). For most semi-pro recording purposes, real cable is stuff like basic **Klotz** and **VDC** – typically around 70 pence a metre.

A three metre jack-to-phono interconnect (the kind you use between mixer and multi-track) with this sort of cable and decent plugs might be around £8, while a ready-made eight-way loom is about £50 – that's £100 for the two sets you'll need to hook up an eight-track system. Then there are effect interconnects, these typically being mono in and stereo out, therefore needing three cables per unit – that's £24 per processor, and potentially far worse if you're going through a patchbay. Also, pity the MIDI user with, say, ten virtual tracks, because that's another £80. The bottom line here is that, though we're talking about what may seem like an appalling amount of money on a pile of totally un-sexy items, quality cables will definitely justify their cost in sonic terms, even with relatively modest gear like high-speed cassette recorders, and it would certainly be false economy to use anything less if you're aiming for release quality from your home studio.

A few words about speaker cables for monitoring: these make a potentially enormous difference to overall sound quality, yet needn't be expensive. There are many hi-fi brands and models, but unless you're prepared to spend much over £5 a metre, your best bet by far is solid-core 'ring-mains' cable (21 amp, 2.5mm²) at about 80 pence a metre from your local electrical wholesaler (check your *Yellow Pages*). The sound quality starts out streets ahead of basic hi-fi products like **QED 79** and **200**, and can be taken a whole league further simply by stripping-off the outer PVC insulating jacket.

Adaptors are best avoided whenever possible, and the worst type of all is generally anything that involves a 'line' (on-cable) jack socket – these tend to be wholly unreliable. If you must buy an adaptor, check out the **Tandy** range, some of whose models are decent quality and realistically

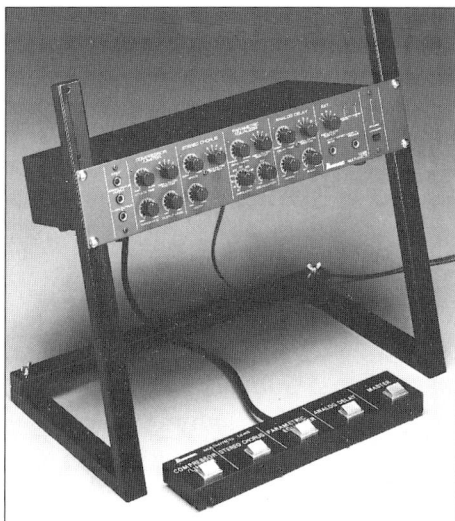

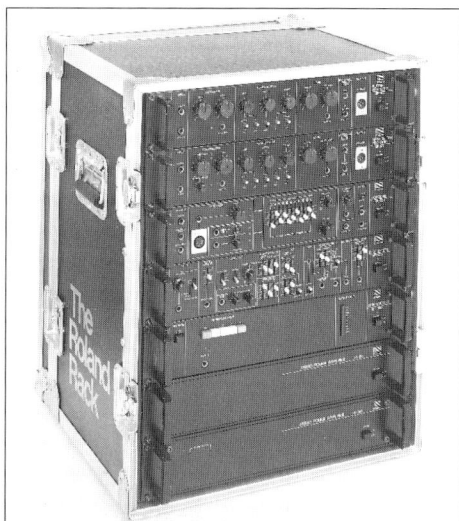

Left: cheap 'n' cheerful Zimmer-style rack from MTR; right: rugged pro flightcase rack

priced. Use all-metal adaptors if available, then accept plastic-bodied ones, and only settle for adaptors using cables if you really can't avoid it.

RACKS AND STANDS

As they say in the biz, 'amateurs stack 'em, pros rack 'em'. Once your effects system gets above about five boxes, you're either going to need a lot of space or a 19-inch rack. Basic racks are quite inexpensive – a 16U job (where 1U equals 1¾in, the height of most rackable FX), might be as little as £75, but once you get down to figuring out where and how you'll use it, you might well be tempted to pay £30-ish extra for my personal favourite, which is an open-frame rack of around 12U, mounted on a stand that provides both height and tilt adjustment. A cheaper variation is the so-called 'Zimmer-frame' rack, providing slightly tilted rack frames which can pack an amazing amount of kit into a small space. But I suggest you think carefully about the 'bending-down' and 'peering-over' implications before committing yourself.

'System stands', which typically provide space for a mixer, computer, nearfield monitors and maybe even a keyboard, are becoming increasingly popular, but though they certainly help a system's visual 'cred', they're also fairly pricey – £200 and more.

The PB-80 patchbay is among many other value-for-money studio accessories from MTR

PATCHBAYS

Sitting in a 19in rack, a patchbay enables you to make all those 'round-the-rear' connections between mixer and effects and back again, but all from the front. This is particularly handy if you want to be able to alter the grouping and order of effects. The basic price of a good quality patchbay isn't usually a problem – maybe £50 for a 32-channel/way job, but remember that decent patch cables cost an extra £4 or so each.

MAINS

Recording set-ups tend to use loads of mains plugs, and the usual solution is to have several four-way distribution boards. This is fine, but if you buy them ready-fitted with mains cable, I urge you to open them up and check that the wiring is tightly screwed down. I have several times encountered distribution boards where the wires were just stuffed into the holes, and not screwed down at all. If you need two or more boards, but have only a single wall socket, don't use those ghastly two/three-way adaptors – plug one board into the wall and up to four extra boards into that.

The most common problem with mains is interference from other equipment, typically in the form of a 'buzzy' click when an item is switched on or off. In extreme cases, the interference can even cause computer crashes. It is possible to put a suppressor on the mains lead of the gear that's causing the problem, but more usual to fit the suppressor to the equipment that's suffering. The price of a suppressor depends partly on how much power it can handle, and a 6A/1500W version will be around £20. Suppressors are not however magic cure-alls, and the ideal is to run a separate mains supply (called a 'spur') direct from your main junction box. The hardware cost of this is peanuts (80 pence a metre for the cable), but the 'real' cost could be vastly greater if you need to hide the cable beneath plaster or run it under floors. Note that a direct spur will avoid interference from other equipment in your house, but won't protect against nasties from outside. A suppressor may help here, but if it doesn't fix the problem, you're in Deep Shit – your electricity board has a theoretical responsibility to ensure your supply is reasonably 'clean', but we're talking about a monopoly, so don't get your hopes up...

Recommended tapes: TDK SA (left) for cassette multi-trackers, HHB for DAT machines

TAPE

High quality tape is vital for high quality sound, and though there's a certain amount of personal preference involved, you won't go far wrong with the following recommendations: **TDK SA** for multi-track cassette machines, **Ampex 456** for the Fostex R8, **456** or **499** for 10½in-reel machines, **TDK** for ADAT and Hi-8, and **HHB** for DAT. This last one may seem strange, but it's based on the 'long-term' tests published in *Studio Sound* magazine, which rated HHB's own-brand well ahead of better-known alternatives. For cassette mixdowns, TDK **SA** is again a good choice, but if your deck can exploit the extra potential of metal tapes (which is not the same as just having a metal position), then try **MA**. Also with cassettes, whether for four-track or stereo, avoid so-called 'super-tapes' (such as SA-X), because they don't conform to the 'standard' tape types for which recorders are (one hopes) correctly set up.

A cassette deck cleaner like Trackmate could be a necessary investment

TAPE RECORDER MAINTENANCE

Most people know that tape recorders need cleaning, and most people do nothing whatever about it, which is why dirty heads are by far the biggest cause of users returning cassette decks to dealers as 'faulty'. For heads and tape guides, you need a pack of Q-tips/cotton buds and a bottle of isopropyl alcohol, but this should never be used for cleaning the black rubber pinch roller, because the alcohol makes it go hard and even crack. You can buy special fluids for this job, but I must confess that I've been using good ol' spit for the past 30 years, and it's never caused any problems. Many cassette decks have appalling access for cleaning – you might find you can manage if you cut the Q-tips in half, but otherwise you'll have to settle for a so-called cassette head cleaner. Many of these are virtually useless, but you'll be fairly safe if you go for a 'wet' rather than 'dry' type from a reputable brand, such as **TDK**, **Allsop** or **Milty**.

Just as physical rubbish builds up on the surface of a head, magnetic rubbish builds up inside it, causing noise and distortion. What's needed is a demagnetiser, and most cassette users can buy one of the highly-convenient 'in-cassette' models (£12-ish, **TDK** and **Milty** again). These are not however suitable for three-head stereo decks or eight-track cassette recorders. For these, and open-reel machines, you need a 'proper' demag, which looks like an overweight soldering iron, and costs from £30 upwards.

SYSTEM PLANNING & BUDGETING

Given a fixed budget, your starting point is to write down every single item you'll need to get to first base. This might be a very short list, as in 'one four-track cassette recorder'; equally it could well run to 50-plus items. Major purchases like mixers and multi-tracks are pretty obvious, but the supposedly 'little' items add up alarmingly, and estimating them realistically is, in my opinion, crucial to cost-effective system planning.

The really difficult part starts when you notice that for many items (major *and* minor), there are several possible products, sometimes at directly comparable prices, and often over a price range. Both situations can make life complicated, so we'll start with resolving 'head-to-head' competitors.

The two most obvious aspects to consider are features and sound quality. To some extent features can be assessed from manufacturers' leaflets, but these understandably only tell you the good news (when did you read a spec that included '*rough* faders' or 'musically *useless* EQ'?). And sound quality can be judged only by trial. So, what we really need is hands-on and ears-on assessment. This kind of stuff takes time, and can work only in a suitable environment (ie, something genuinely credible in the way of monitoring – short of studio-style gear, a serious full-range PA – and no guitarist murdering 'Stairway' 15 feet away).

You'll need something to play through whatever it is you're trying out, and precisely what you need depends as much on what equipment you're testing as on your style of music. It seems logical to start at the beginning of the recording chain – with **microphones** – and immediately we're in deep water. Sing and/or play into mikes, but don't try to judge on cans – record your mini-performance, then listen on speakers. Remember that a mike has more than just a single on-axis/straight-in-front character; its sound will vary at different angles and distances – aspects that could potentially be very important, both as problems and opportunities (see *Miking Up*).

Testing **mixers** is quite difficult – most modern semi-pro jobs achieve a sound quality best described as adequate, and none really stand out from the crowd on this score. So, given that a desk has sufficient channels, groups, sends and returns, it's all down to overall 'feel' and the effectiveness of the EQ. The problem with 'feel' is that it's all very well to talk about how easily you can find and set things like sends, but this kind of stuff inevitably involves a 'learning curve', so a desk that seems a bugger to begin with might

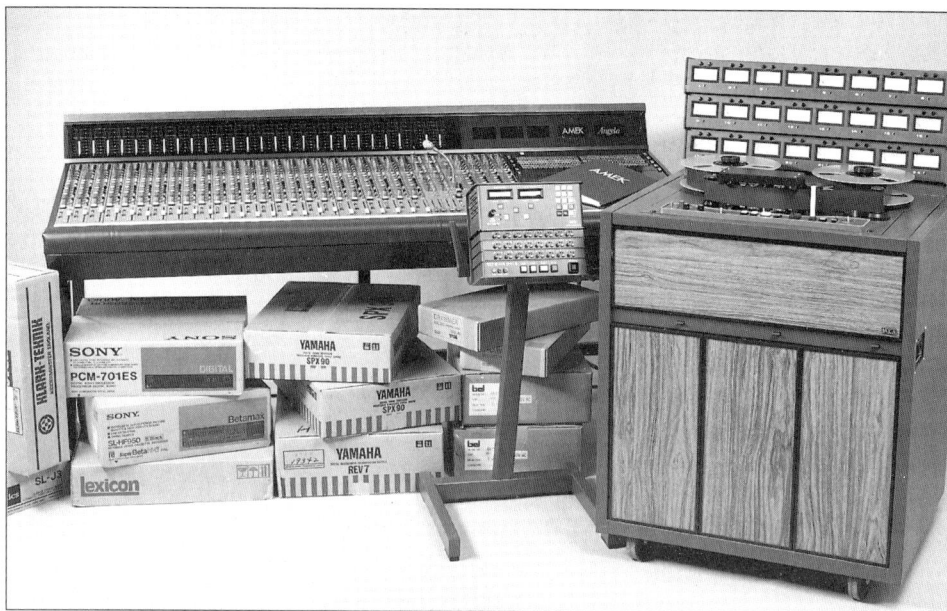

Your plans for a system could be a very short list, as in 'one four-track cassette recorder', or something a little more ambitious, like this system HHB put together for producer Steve Lillywhite a few years back. The then state-of-the-art set-up comprised an Amek Angela 28-into-24 desk, Sony/MCI JH2424 24-track recorder with autolocator, Sony PCM 701ES, Sony SL-HF950 Betamax recorder for digital use, two Yamaha SPX-90 multi-effects units, one Yamaha REV 7 digital reverb, two Drawmer DS201 noise gates, two Bel BD 240 DDLs, one Klark-Teknik DM3322 graphic and one Lexicon PCM 70 digital reverb. Wonder how much of it is still in use now...

well be a piece of cake after a couple of weeks' use (and, then again, it might not...). To test EQ, you need a tape of the kind of things you'll be recording. The really vital point is that the track should be audibly in need of EQ – something that doesn't need EQ is hardly likely to demonstrate the benefits of the stuff.

What could be called **'performance' effects** (such as most guitar boxes) are best tested simply by plugging them in, playing some music on your regular instrument(s), experimenting with what they can do, and paying attention to how easily you can get them to do it. Unfortunately, life ain't so simple if it's an effect you'll be using on several instruments at once – most obviously and commonly, reverb. Try it on individual instruments by all means, but you may well find that you need both different amounts of reverb for different sources (no problem if your mixer has effect sends) and different reverb programs. This latter is a swine, because the only ways out are: settle for a compromise program (as in Jack of all trades but master of none), play the dangerous game of recording 'wet' (see *Working With Effects*), or buy *two* reverbs. Depending on the music, I find that having more than one reverb can make real contributions to the production quality, certainly to the point where you could consider having two £200 units rather than one £400 box. Note that all the above points also apply to compressors.

Testing a **recorder** is fairly straightforward if you have the right source material: dbx naughties are most easily revealed by solo bass drum or vocals, while slow piano and acoustic guitar should show up wow and flutter. As an overall test, any well-recorded CD will reveal how much general quality loss occurs, though of course you'll only be able to hear this with decent monitoring and a quiet environment.

All of the above should aid you in comparing like with like, but doesn't do much to help you decide how to divide your total budget among the various items you need. Some aspects are largely common sense: an £800 microphone with a four-track cassette recorder would be overkill, while a £100 mike with ADAT might be underkill (depending on what you're recording). But effects, for example, are not so simple, and only you can decide whether you're happy with the sound of cheapish units. You can read reviews, though these usually only comment on sound quality if it's either really grim or really great. You can ask retailers, though in my experience, few of them are happy to make judgement calls, and there's always the suspicion that the advice you're getting might just be influenced by the state of the stock cupboard and the profit margins.

Probably the most important piece of advice is to buy only from a dealer who will offer you 'sale or return' – this is where you pay for the gear, then have a week or so to try it out at home. A variation on this theme is where you pay a hire charge, which is then deducted from the bill if you decide to buy. Some retailers go a whiter shade of deathly at the mere suggestion of sale or return, in which case I personally would take my custom elsewhere. Bear in mind that, if you buy any item by mail-order, the Code of Advertising Practice gives you a minimum of seven days home approval, and if you pay for mail-ordered goods by credit/debit card, the card company will back you up should the retailer be unhappy with a return-for-refund request.

Feel free to negotiate on price – 'official' retail is often a work of highly-hopeful fiction, and even advertised 'discount deals' can often be bettered with a little hands-on haggling. If price is critical to you, expect to do some phoning round – importers and manufacturers are forever doing deals with retailers, so it may take a while to locate the dealer who can offer the best price.

SECONDHAND

Everyone likes a bargain, and buying secondhand can open the door to some big-time bargains. Unfortunately, it can also open the door to some big-time disasters. So, the name of the game is getting the bargain without getting bitten – and this process starts with who you buy from. There are three main sources...

Most retailers deal in secondhand gear, usually stuff they've taken in part-exchange. Because he's a professional, a dealer has to ensure that what he sells is of 'merchantable quality', which basically means that it does what it's supposed to. Also, he has to guarantee it for a 'reasonable period', which is generally taken to mean a minimum of three months. On the one hand, these safeguards should make buying from a dealer your safest bet; on the other, you'll almost always end up paying for the privilege – dealer prices may be 70 percent of the new price.

The second source is to buy from a friend. Hopefully this means that he'll tell you about any aspects of the gear that are 'iffy', and the price will probably be not much more than half the new retail, perhaps quite a bit less, depending on condition and your friend's desperation for dosh. Most such deals work out well, but there's one point that you and your friend should be certain to sort out before money changes hands, and that is just who will be responsible for what, if the gear breaks down soon (whatever that means) after purchase – otherwise you could end up with a broken thingy *and* a broken friendship. (My own opinion is that there should be no guarantee at all – in the heat of doing a deal, it's easy enough for the seller to say he'll guarantee the item, but another thing entirely when you rock up three days later and announce that it's exploded, burnt your house down, and you'd like £50,000 please, preferably before the banks shut...)

The final secondhand source is also by far the riskiest, and that's ads in music magazines, the countless 'free-ad' papers, *Exchange & Mart*, and on dealers' noticeboards. Some sellers have wildly unrealistic ideas about price, but even when the asking price looks fair, there is absolutely no way you should even entertain the notion unless you or a friend really know your techno-stuff.

Whoever you're buying from, you'll probably want to make a few basic checks, and what follows gives you the main points to look for. But beware, just as it's possible to make a dying car gearbox seem OK by mixing a

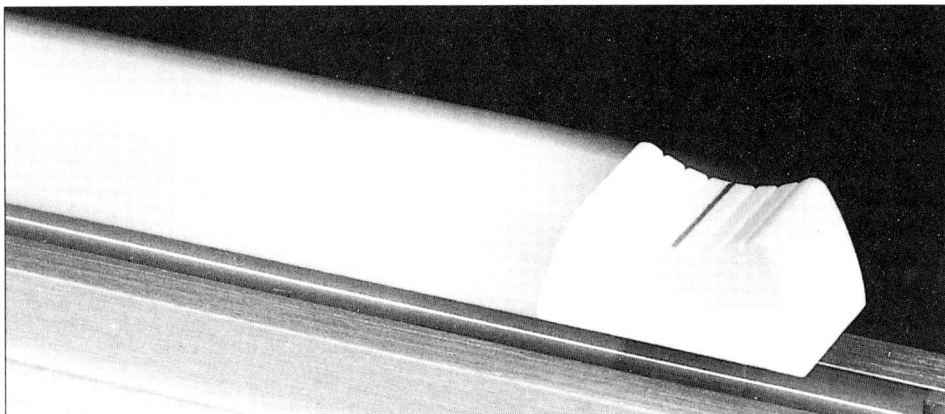

A noisy fader can be temporarily turned into a silent glider with a squirt of WD-40

little sawdust in with the oil, a quick spray of Servisol or WD-40 will soon silence a noisy fader – or at least, it will until the seller is safely out of range.

Whatever the specific item of gear, your best overall guide is its general condition – a scratch might indicate just an isolated accident, but be especially wary of worn control markings, a sure sign that the gear's seen plenty of use.

Checking out a mixer is a fairly time-consuming process, simply because there are so many knobs, switches and connectors, any of which could be naff. To do the job thoroughly, you really need a mike, a line-level source (CD or tape), a pair of cans, and a hi-fi amp. Starting with channel one and group one, you first want to get a signal through the desk; then, with the volume whacked up on cans, work your way through all the controls listening for any 'dead-spots' where the sound disappears. Then repeat the process, but without the test signal playing – this time you're on the lookout for excessive hum or hiss, and particularly, any crackles or spluttering when using knobs or faders. Bear in mind that you'll need to switch the monitors to check effect and foldback sends. Repeat the process for each channel, then check all the groups. The fact that a signal is getting through to the phones monitor doesn't always guarantee that it's also coming out of whatever output(s) it ought to, which is where you connect your amp and use it to drive the cans.

Effect processors are fairly similar to mixers in terms of checking,

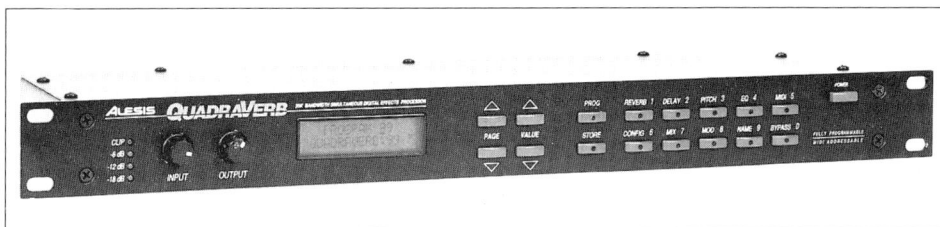

Checking procedure for a secondhand effects processor is like a simplified mixer check

but usually far simpler. Mikes, amps, speakers and phones are also quite straightforward – listen for hum, hiss, loss of signal, buzzes, rattles, distortion, and any missing part(s) of the sound spectrum.

The real trouble comes with recorders, whether they be separate or part of a multi-track cassette machine. Naturally, you need to check that each track records, plays back, and erases. Next, listen to the transport itself – do all the functions engage and disengage smoothly? Does it make any irregular noises when running? (A slight 'swish' is normal, but it should be smooth.) Does it wind the tape evenly, both when playing and fast-spooling? Take a look at the pinch wheel (that's the rubber item to the right of the heads): the rubber should be black; a brown stain the width of the tape says it hasn't been cleaned properly.

So far so good; but the real question now arises – is the record/play head OK? This is both important and difficult – important because a dead head means no treble, and a new head is a mighty pricey item (over £150 for a

With recorders, it's vital that the record/play tape head is OK; replacing one is very costly

budget Porta, £500-ish for an eight-track, and well over a grand for a 16-track). With prices like these, you really don't want to get caught out. Problem is that a head may seem to be working perfectly, but only have a few months' life left (rather like the way alkaline batteries deliver full power until almost the very end). You can try examining the head closely – as a head is used, a small 'flat' develops across the centre (where the all-important gaps are). If this flat is only about a millimetre wide, you're probably OK – anything over two mil and you should run a mile. If the head is sharply curved, as on some cassette machines, then the tolerances are much less; also, in such cases, you've got the problem of actually seeing the head – what you really need here is a dental mirror. Doubtless this is just the sort of item you carry all the time, but if not, some tape head cleaning kits include them.

Rather like a rebore on a car engine, it is possible to get heads 're-lapped' – this is cheaper than a new head, but may not last as long.

Another check is to record and play back a signal with lots of treble, in which case use the outermost tracks. The only remaining approach is to make a guess based on how old the recorder is, and how much use it may have seen. Estimates of head-life vary wildly, but 2000–4000 hours is probably a reasonable ballpark. Trouble is, you may not know whether the thing's been used once a week or ten hours a day. Quite frankly, unless you know the owner, you might just as well flip a coin...

SELLING SECONDHAND

Assuming that whatever you're selling works properly, your best bet by far is to flog it to a friend. A dealer's offer is likely to be disappointing, even if you're buying something in part-exchange – 40 percent of the new price would generally be good going. Your only other option is to advertise, but be warned, this can turn into a real nightmare – strange phone calls at 2am, people who fix a time to come round then don't show up (usually when you've taken the day off work), people who say they'll be round with the money tomorrow, then disappear after you've turned away two other buyers, people who roll up expecting a five-hour recording tutorial...

If you do decide to advertise, there are four golden rules: check what other advertisers are asking for similar gear (not that it means you'll get it, only that you won't get *any* calls at all if you overprice), be prepared to haggle at least ten percent off the starting price, get the phone number of every enquirer (in case a deal falls through or you decide to drop your price), and never take a cheque without hanging onto the goods until it's cleared.

PART TWO
PRACTICAL RECORDING

ENGINEERING & PRODUCTION

Production often involves a lot of pre-planning before you get to the creative mixing bit

Talking in the most general terms, a producer is someone who knows *what* they want to do, and an engineer is someone who knows *how* to do it. Unless you're using a commercial studio, or you're splitting the work with another musician, you'll usually be both engineer and producer.

This actually has its advantages, because there shouldn't be any 'communication problems'. But having a separate person as producer has its plus points too: they'll hopefully bring a broad range of experience with them, and be able to judge both music and sound with a sense of 'perspective' that a composer-muso may lack (something about 'seeing the wood for the trees'). In the case of a band, the producer can also act as a kind of 'independent mediator' when disagreements/ego-conflicts/fights break out.

Producer-type work often starts long before recording, and what's most relevant here is 'track planning', which in many cases comes with its depressing sidekick, 'bounce planning'. Your starting point is to make a list of every musical element, and the order in which you'd like to record them. Even this can pose problems, because a lot of musos like to work 'on-the-fly', so you may have only a few basic ideas at this stage – all you can do is plan-in the opportunity to add tracks further down the line. If you're working with virtual tracks and analogue tape, you'll need to allow for the sync track, and if not, you may want a 'click track' to define the tempo, or, at the least, a 'click' intro on the drum track(s) to ensure that all the tracks start off in-time.

Most recordists want to lay down the rhythm section first, and this usually means drums and bass; these might be recorded at the same time, or one after the other. In a pro environment (where pro equals loadsa tracks), you'd almost certainly record a 'guide vocal' next, though it's only really useful if you, or other musos, are going to record further accompaniment tracks before the vocal 'proper'. Speaking of which, you might, if you've got the tracks, like to think about allocating two for the lead vocals. This has two potential advantages: it makes vocal 'drop-ins' (see *Laying Down Tracks*) far easier, and also allows you to 'overlap' vocals, the most common example being where the last syllable of a verse overlaps with the first syllable of the chorus. (If tracks permit, you might want to also consider using two for, say, lead guitar.)

From here on, the working order may be anybody's guess, but if your recording will involve bouncing, the order you'd musically like to record in may well have to take second place to consideration of what elements you need to bounce together. Bearing in mind the problems of bounce mixing, it's best to try and plan things so you bounce items that 'fit' together musically, the most obvious example being the rhythm section. Another point is the potential to do stereo rather than mono bounces. This is particularly attractive with drums, but also potentially with backing vocals, stereo keyboards, and just about any arrangement that involves bouncing two similar instruments 'playing off' each other (as in, two lead guitars exchanging riffs). Stereo bouncing is usually straightforward with eight tracks, but equally-commonly a problem with four. As you plan this, remember that, if your hands aren't tied-up on the mixer during bouncing, you can add another instrument 'live'.

Once you've figured all these aspects out for your particular production, you can put together a 'track sheet', with track numbers down the left, and next to each a brief description of what will be on the track. Sync will conventionally be on the highest-numbered track, and if lack of tracks means you can't leave a 'guard track' next to it, try to use that track for something that has a limited dynamic range and/or will not be prominent in the final mix. You can draw arrows on the track sheet to indicate what will be bounced to where, and brackets for stereo pairs. With open-reel, try to use the outermost tracks for backing rather than lead elements (so that any drop-outs are less noticeable).

With a complex production, especially one which may take place over weeks or months, this track sheet can become a marginally vital piece of paper – your plans may well change as a production evolves, but provided you keep the track sheet up-to-date, it not only tells you 'what's where' track-wise, but what you've done, where you've got to, and what's still to come. The moral is simple: keep the track sheet with the multitrack master tape at all times. Use a pencil and keep an eraser handy.

Another potential aspect of track and bounce planning involves effects. As we'll see in *Working With Effects*, the ideal is almost always to leave adding them until the mixdown stage. This is fine theory, but not always practicable – the worst case is where all your effects come from a single multi-effect box, but you want different effects on different tracks. The same kind of problem can also happen with separate effect units, and you need to plan what effect(s) you'll want, both for specific track(s), and for the final stereo mix. This may reveal that you need to record and/or bounce tracks 'wet' (with effects), which is definitely worth knowing in advance.

Once you get down to actual recording, the single most important rôle of the producer is time management. This possibly sounds seriously boring, but it's potentially very significant – things like knowing when to abandon work on a track that won't come right, and knowing when to say, "Yeah, that'll do; it's probably as good as we'll get this side of Christmas." We're not just talking about saving time here, but also maintaining a productive psychological mood.

MIKING UP

Cardioids like this Shure are the most commonly used mikes

The art and craft of effective miking is one of those contrary subjects that manages to be both simple and extremely complex – simple in that we can get all the basics into just a few pages; complex in that some engineers are paid quite large sums of money just for knowing how to get the desired results quickly and easily. We'll start with some general points that apply in almost all situations...

It probably won't come as any surprise that, in most cases, you point the business end of the mike at the business end of whatever it's miking – the bit the sound comes out of. Which raises the obvious question of just how close or far apart the mike and instrument should be. As you'll know from the *Microphones* chapter, the most commonly used mike is a cardioid/uni-directional type, and one of its properties is the 'proximity effect' which produces unavoidable bass boost as you bring sound source and mike closer together. This actually occurs as far as two feet apart, and by six inches we're talking about up to 15dB of boost – the equivalent of turning a bass control up to full. Things may not be quite this bad in practice, because the mike designer will have balanced the frequency response to be flat(ish) at a certain distance, commonly 12 inches. Depending on your EQ facilities, you may be able to counteract the boom that results from closer working, but in most cases it's better to keep the mike at least six to nine inches away from the target.

As you move the mike further away, two important things happen: you pick up more of the room's natural reverb (which may or may not be what you want), and you also pick up more of whatever other instruments are playing in the room (almost certainly something you don't want).

Even the apparently straightforward concept of pointing the mike at the sound source can get complicated – the two most obvious problem cases are where the instrument itself is physically large, or where it may be moved around while being played. The size problem is especially obvious with, say, a piano – if you want an upfront/close-in sound, the mike will inevitably be much closer to some strings than others, which in turn will affect their relative loudness.

One answer here is to use two mikes, though this brings in a whole new ballgame called 'phase additions and cancellations', which is where some notes and/or harmonics become artificially louder or quieter; the only solution here is very careful fine-tuning of the two mikes' positions. The 'moving instrument problem' is most easily demonstrated by a saxophone – have you ever seen a saxophonist who holds his instrument completely stationary while playing? Me neither. Just about the only answer is to provide the musician with plenty of foldback, so he can hear how movement affects pick-up of both loudness and tone, and use the effects creatively. Alternatively this is where some people reach for a clip-on mike.

Further thoughts: unless you know that a particular mike needs a certain kind of EQ whatever it's used on, you'll generally do better to fine-tune the mike's position rather than trying to 'cook' the sound with EQ. Bear in mind that any mike's tonal character/frequency response varies at different angles – with a cardioid, you might sacrifice sensitivity, but prefer the tone with sideways pick-up. Also, if you still can't get the kind of sound you want even with a little EQ, try another microphone (easier said than afforded).

Having made quite a fuss about the Tandy PZM back in *Microphones*, we'll give its use a separate section, but first we'll look in some detail at miking up using conventional mikes...

VOCALS

With 'stick-type' moving-coils, point the mike straight down at the floor. This has three advantages over the more normal 'live-performance' upwards-facing position: nasal breathing effects will be aimed at where the mike is least sensitive; room reverb will be reduced (assuming the floor is carpeted); and the vocalist will be singing across the mike rather than straight into it, which greatly reduces the chance of two major potential nasties: 'popping' 'plosive' pees and bees (which come out as a kind of *'puh'* and *'buh'* effect), and sibilant esses.

Some condensers are stick-types, in which case, treat them as above, but others have the element facing sideways – if you sing straight into it, you'll very possibly need a 'pop' windshield, though you may be able to get

Popper stopper: posher windshield than old stocking

away without one if you change your position to about 45 degrees to one side.

The main problem with vocal miking isn't usually anything to do with the mike or its position, but difficulties with vocal technique. The main culprit here is when the vocalist wanders closer to/away from the mike, which can produce dramatic changes in volume. Normal singing itself involves expressive volume changes, and these alone can be enough to create problems when trying to place the vocals in the mix, which is why a compressor is almost universally used on vocals. But over-compression creates a highly-unnatural 'dead' sound, so a singer who fails to keep a constant distance from the mike just makes matters worse by increasing the amount of compression that's needed. A windshield can help, by at least ensuring that the singer doesn't get too close to the mike; also try making the vocals fairly loud in the foldback mix.

ELECTRIC GUITAR
By far the simplest technique is not to use a mike at all, but to feed the guitar signal, or the output from your effect box(es), straight into the mixer (known as DI, for direct injection/insertion). This gives the cleanest, most accurate sound (especially if you use a dedicated DI box), but this may not be at all what you want. Many guitarists regard their amp and speaker as an essential and integral part of creating their 'sound', which is perfectly reasonable. Some modern guitar multi-effects units feature one or even several 'speaker simulators', which is fine if they give the tonal effects you want, but many axe-people still reckon you can't beat the real thing. So...

Put the guitar combo on a chair or stool, with a towel betwixt the two to discourage buzzes, and aim your mike straight at the centre of the speaker cone, from about nine inches away. Record a test track and listen on your monitor speakers (rather than playing live into phones). If the result is too toppy, turn the mike so it's facing the edge of the speaker cone. If you want more bass, move the whole set-up so that the combo's back is only a couple of inches away from a wall, or put it on the floor – or both. And if you want to get creative, try tricks like mixing-in the signal from a second mike actually inside the back of the combo, or from about five feet in front. You could, of course, mix in a little DI as well.

ELECTRIC BASS
In principle, you can mike a bass combo much like an ordinary one, but there can be fairly serious problems. You may not notice it much when playing normally, but if you listen carefully, you'll often find that some notes come out distinctly louder than others, which will lead to difficulties when placing the bass in the final mix. These problems can be caused by the guitar, strings, and pick-ups, but the major culprit is usually the speaker, which seldom has a completely flat frequency response. The answer here is definitely DI, though maybe with a 'speaker simulator' effect.

ACOUSTIC GUITAR
Simply place a mike nine inches away from the body, and pointing into the sound-hole. If you want less body resonance and more string twang, angle the mike more towards the neck, but bear in mind that this will emphasise mechanical and handling noises, like squeaks and fret buzz.

ELECTRO-ACOUSTIC GUITAR
You're completely spoilt for choice here – you can mike the guitar itself, mike the combo, use DI, or try any combination of the three. As with most mikey things, when it sounds right, it is.

ACOUSTIC BASS

Pretty much the same as an ordinary acoustic, except that I'd be strongly tempted to use a vocal-type mike – the 'presence' boost will help minimise the chances of the bass coming over as just a dull boom.

DRUMS

OK, we may as well face it from the start: drums are the cause of more miking headaches than probably all other instruments put together. There are two root causes. First, a drumkit isn't just a single instrument – even a fairly small kit may well have ten or more separate items. Worse, these instruments between them cover the full frequency range from deepest bass to highest treble.

It is perfectly possible to mike each drum and cymbal separately, and such a set-up has the potential advantages that you can pan bits of the

Michael Witzel miked-up for Chris de Burgh session

kit to any points you like on the stereo soundstage, and also apply effects selectively (such as gating on snare). Desirable it may be, but practical it often isn't, simply because of the number of mikes needed. So instead, we'll start with the most basic set-up of all – a single mike. What we need here is to get the mike far enough away for it to capture all the elements of the kit without favouritism. You could do this by putting the mike five or six feet in front of the kit, but miking from above is much more common. Place a boom stand behind the drummist, and bring the boom arm in over his/her head, so the mike is above, and pointing directly at, the point where the snare drum is closest to the side toms. Given a decent mike, this will generally produce acceptable results, though the bass drum is likely to be woolly and lacking impact. The only known cure is a second mike, in front of, or preferably inside, the bass drum – as close to the beater's point of impact as possible to maximise 'smack' (and use a mike that can cope with very high sound levels).

The above set-up gives us only mono drums, which is something you may have to settle for if you're fourtracking. But stereo is vastly preferable, simply because that's what we've come to expect from commercial recordings. Still avoiding miking everything separately, all we do is replace the single overhead mike with a pair, one above the hi-hat, the other over the floor tom, and maybe angle both in slightly, so they're halfway pointing towards the snare drum. Note that you'll still need a separate mike for the bass drum.

This kind of miking can give very good results indeed, but if you're still not happy, it may well be the snare that needs attention. The answer is a fourth mike, either above or beneath the drum. If you place it above, it will have to be close to the edge to avoid being hit accidentally, and this will produce a fairly lightish tone. From underneath, you can get it right in the middle of the head, which will give much more depth, but also accentuate snare resonance. Some professional engineers swear by miking both above and below – this is fine if you've got enough mikes.

PIANO

As I observed at the start of this chapter, pianos can be tricky things. With uprights, life is a lot easier if you leave the front in place, since it acts as a diffuser, and largely avoids the problem of some strings being closer to the mike than others. Either way, you should generally mike from two, preferably three feet away, and slightly above the pianist's head. You could also try using two mikes, again from a couple of feet, one at the bass end and one at the treble, but each pointing towards the opposite end.

Grand pianos might seem really difficult, but they can actually pose fewer problems than uprights. Place a cardioid/uni about halfway down the length of the piano, and about two foot beyond the side-edge. By pointing the mike sideways (towards the bass end), the treble strings won't be overpowering, because the bass will be reinforced by the lid. Depending on the tone you want, move the mike closer to/further from the hammers (ie up/down the length of the piano). And, if you fancy a really rich flavour, add a second mike actually underneath the piano.

ELECTRIC ORGAN

Miking a modern electric is basically similar to a guitar combo, except that many organs use separate bass/mid and treble speakers, so you have to experiment with position to get the tonal balance you're after (beware of hiss if you put the mike directly in front of the treble drive unit). The practical problem here is that the speakers may well be obstructed by the organist's knees (for which the obvious cure is amputation). Traditional electric organs often use external speakers, the all-time classic being the Leslie, with its rotating mid/treble unit. You'll need two mikes for this, one in front of the bass, the second about six inches in front of and above the treble. If you really want to go to town, use two mikes on the treble, one either side, and pan them to left and right in the stereo mix (the bass mike goes centre-stage).

STRINGS
Mike from about nine inches above the sound-hole and slightly to one side, or use a contact mike for a really upfront 'wiry' sound.

BRASS
Aren't trumpets *loud*? Yes, they are, so if you need to get in close, be sure to use a mike that can cope; just point it towards the bell from about nine inches away.

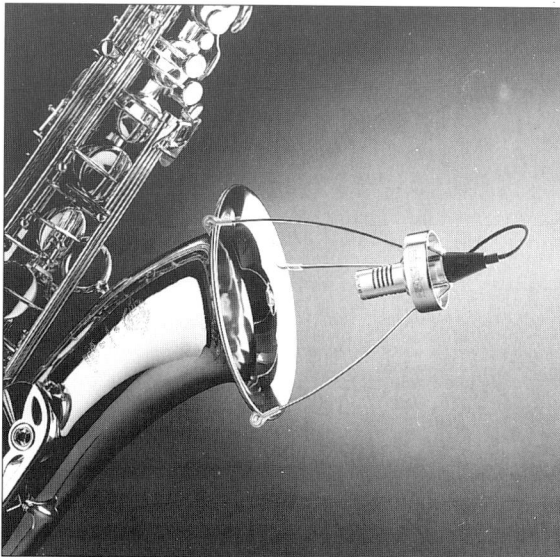

SD Systems' answer to saxophone miking problems

WIND
Again, nine inches is the golden rule, but this time, keep the mike well to one side to avoid excessive breathiness.

OTHER INSTRUMENTS
Follow the general guidelines at the beginning of this chapter and, as ever, take time to experiment.

TANDY PZM

If what you want is a 'natural' sound, then it's almost impossible to go wrong with the PZM – once you solve the problem of what to mount it on. BluTacking or gaffer-taping it to a wall is the obvious solution, except that both BluTack and gaffer tape are highly effective at stripping paint and even wallpaper. You can sometimes get away with just dumping it on the floor, but the easiest and best solution is to pop it on a large table-top (assuming you've

For a 'natural' sound, you can hardly go wrong with a Tandy PZM

got a large table). Alternatively, you could get a four-foot square mounting panel for it – hardboard is cheap and cheerful, but can cause boom; quarter-inch perspex is pricey but preferable.

Most instruments will sound best at a distance of a couple of feet, possibly a little closer for vocals (which happen to sound rather good on the PZM, though some musos find singing into it a 'weird' experience). Because the PZM has a hemispherical pick-up pattern, it isn't much use where you want to isolate one instrument from surrounding sounds, but by the same token, it's first-rate when you *do* want to capture several instruments with just a single mike.

To use the PZM as a contact mike, just undo the two screws that secure the mounting plate to the business bit; you can then attach it to your instrument with double-sided sticky tape (but check first, using an unseen part of the body, that the tape won't damage the laquer finish). The only practical drawback to using the PZM as a contact mike is that its cable isn't detachable – short of unsticking and resticking the mike, it, and the cable, are there to stay.

LAYING DOWN TRACKS

First step is to clear the controls – about as much fun as cleaning tape heads, but vital

If you're completely new to recording, what you're probably looking for here is a 'virgin's guide' to exactly what needs inserting, pushing, turning and tweaking, and in what order. Sadly, this is not to be, simply because there are so many variations in the features of recording hardware, and in how those features actually work. You'll find the 'press-this-to-do-that' stuff in your instruction manual(s), though I can't actually vouch for how intelligible the contents may be – some manuals are excellent, others are near-gibberish (which is where it's handy if your hopefully-knowledgeable dealer is only a local-rate/freephone call away). What this chapter does is describe the steps in the process of recording, though to keep things reasonably straightforward, I'm ignoring 'details' like recording timecode/sync or a click track (see *Engineering And Production*).

STEP ONE – CLEAR THE CONTROLS

This is about as much fun as cleaning tape heads, but just as important. Set the gain/trims, sends and faders to minimum, EQ to flat (0), and record selectors to off/'safe'. Depending on where you're up to in a particular production, you may also want to turn down track monitors and/or effect returns. The idea behind all of this is to 'undo' everything that's been done to date (except items like a track monitor mix that you specifically want to keep), and the justification for being bothered is that, if you don't, Sod's Law will sooner or later creep up on you, with deeply dissatisfying results like erasing a track that's just taken you two hours to get right, or recording an (unwanted) foldback mix along with the wanted track. These things do happen.

STEP TWO – GET SOME SOUND

The first thing is to get the right plug into the right socket and, if you're using a microphone, set a rough position using *Miking Up* as a guide. With DIed guitar, you can use a mike/line input, but tone will be better with a DI box (also avoiding potential phantom power problems – see *Mixer Features*). If your guitar is running through one or more effect boxes, there should be plenty of level to drive a line in.

The next step is to route the signal from the input through to the desired recorder track (as shown on the appropriate meter), and to the monitors ('phones or speakers). This may be as simple as pushing a couple of buttons on a cassette multi-track, but much more complicated on a multi-group desk. Bring faders up, starting at the recorder end of the signal path, setting them to 0dB (7–8), then finally play the source and slowly turn up the channel gain/trim.

At which point, all sorts of things may, or may not, happen. If there's no audible or visible signal, work through from input to recorder and monitors – check group routing and monitor selection; on some cassette multi-tracks you may need to switch to 'record pause' to get a meter reading. Use the gain/trim to set a rough recorder level (around 0dB peaks for analogue, -12 for digital).

If you need cue/foldback from previously-recorded tracks, add this to the monitor mix.

STEP THREE – TWEAK THE SOUND

With a miked source, this process starts with microphone position. This can be difficult if you're playing as well as engineering, and the answer is to record a few 'test tracks' while you experiment with the mike. This kind of fiddle is a real turn-off when you're on a creative roll, so it's a good idea to play with miking up when you're not recording seriously – once you've found the best position, memory or an index card will allow you to recreate the sound at will.

Except for a lo-cut filter to reduce possible bass rubbish, don't even think about adding EQ until you've done your damnedest to get the sound you want by mike placement – even the best EQ is really quite crude compared to the differences created by miking. If you end up deciding that you do want EQ, it's worth considering whether you really need to add it at the track-recording stage, rather than leaving it till bounce/mixdown time. If you're both playist and recordist, it makes sense to record a short 'test track' without EQ, then explore the EQ on playback, finally transferring the settings you choose to the 'live' channel.

If you're recording 'wet' (with effects), now's the time to add them. Professionals usually keep both EQ and effects to a minimum at this stage, but as we saw in *Engineering And Production*, hardware restrictions may force you to do some effects work during initial recording. As with EQ, you may well find it easier to use a test track for effect-setting.

STEP FOUR – SET THE FINAL LEVEL

This is easy to describe, but potentially quite tricky in practice – you want the highest-possible level to minimise hiss (especially with analogue), but not so high that an unexpected peak causes overload distortion to ruin an otherwise perfect take. With cassette, I would tend to set the peak level to around 0dB (leaving about 5dB of 'headroom'), with open-reel maybe +3 (about 7dB headroom), and about -10/12dB for digital (10/12dB headroom). If there are any outboard effects, check their meters. Zero the tape counter.

One last check: without playing, and using 'phones rather than speakers, whack the monitor volume up really high, then listen for hums, buzzes, crackles or hiss. The first two might be cured by moving the input cable around, or, along with crackles, they might be caused by the cable itself being dodgy. Hiss usually indicates either that signal levels, though right by the time they get to the recorder meters, are well down somewhere along the line (perhaps an inserted effect), or that an unused and unwanted channel/group/buss in/aux return is feeding into the record signal.

STEP FIVE – GO FOR IT

Not much to say, is there? Yes, there's plenty to say, but it's more about music than recording – the important point is that, if you've followed all of the above, you can safely forget about the recording side completely, and concentrate on the music. This is as it should be. Two practical points: if the track is going to end with a fadeout, play at least four bars beyond the expected end of the fade. And if you're not fading out, try to keep still and therefore quiet for at least four or five seconds after the last note dies away – it's amazing how many home productions end with a beautifully-recorded chair creak...

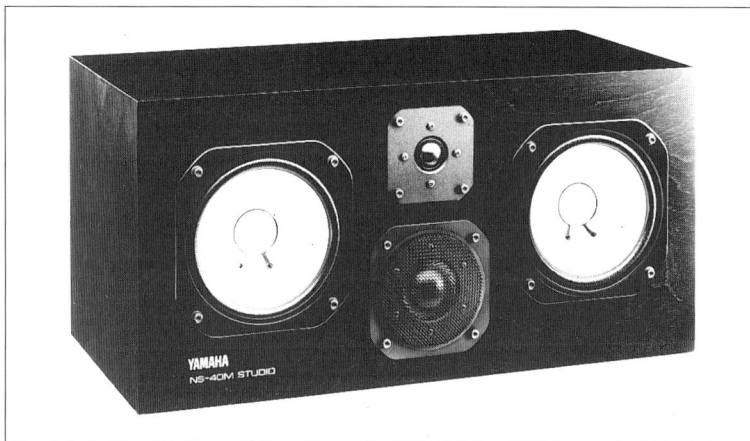

Listen to each track on its own, then monitor mixed to see how it fits in

STEP SIX – LISTEN

Set the record selector(s) to off/safe, rewind to zero, and set the mixer so you can hear what you've just recorded. You'll probably want to hear it two different ways – on its own, to listen for any fluffs, and monitor-mixed with previous tracks to see how it fits in. If you're happy, it's time to update the track sheet (see *Engineering And Production*) with a little tick, return to step one, and start work on the next track. But if you're not happy, it may be either the sound or some aspect of the playing that's not right. If it's the sound, you can try correcting it with EQ and/or effects, but with the playing, life can be more difficult. If you realise that one of your guitar strings was out of tune, you don't have much choice but to record again; if however the problem is, say, just one bum note, you may prefer to consider...

STEP SEVEN – THE DREADED DROP-IN

All multi-tracks have facilities for drop-ins/punch-ins, enabling you to play back a track and, at the critical moment, drop-in to record, play the wrong bit right, then drop-out again, leaving the rest of the track intact. Sounds great, doesn't it?

The reality is not so simple. Some recorders, notably many cassette multi-tracks, put a nice little click on the tape both when entering and leaving record mode. Also, with any analogue recorder, there's a time-lapse between a point on the tape passing the erase head and its reaching the record/play head. This has two effects: at the start of a drop-in, you hit 'record' at the end of the last original note you want to keep, but the erase head is working a split-second ahead, so it very probably doesn't erase the start of the first note you want to replace. The result can be a Right Mess, with both old and new versions of the same note on the track. And then, when you've finished your drop-in, you drop-out at the end of the last new note, but once again the erase head is that split-second in front, so it will quite likely have erased part of the next note from the original take. These problems get worse if you're recording with reverb, because it's almost impossible to avoid chopping-off the original reverb when you drop-in, and the new reverb when you drop-out.

The usual advice for minimising these problems is to plan your 'in' and 'out' points so that they occur at the end of musical phrases. This is fine if you've got such 'natural breaks', but not much use otherwise. Another frequently offered helpful hint is to start playing well before the drop-in point, so that you 'get into the groove' and, rather importantly, match volumes with the previous take. Again, life ain't necessarily so simple – with acoustic instruments, it can be very off-putting to hear your live version at the same time as the existing track.

As you'll have gathered, I'm not a great fan of drop-ins, mostly because I've many times seen people devote vast amounts of effort to getting them right, only to end up accepting that they really need to do the whole track again. Equally, I have to admit that there are times when drop-ins can be jolly useful, especially with vocals. Even here though, a drop-in is often a poor substitute for having two vocal tracks, but this may not be a practical option with four- or eight-track systems, and anyway makes for more work at mixdown time.

WORKING WITH EFFECTS

Before we get down to the joys of knob-twiddling, we have to figure out how to hook our effect processor(s) into our recording system. This might seem like simplicity itself, but it turns out that there are actually no less than five different ways – I'll describe them briefly, and then look at their applications.

IN-LINE
The effect processor goes between the instrument and the input to the recording system. This is the way guitarists generally use their effect pedals, though there's no reason why it can't be used for keyboards or even drum boxes – just about the only restriction is that you can't generally work this way with microphones, because very few processors have mike-level inputs.

OUT-LINE
The processor goes between the output of the main recording system and the inputs to the stereo master deck and/or monitoring system. This can be highly convenient, but there are two points to bear in mind: we're dealing with stereo signals, so the processor will need stereo inputs and outputs; also, and very importantly, all the elements in the mix will receive the same dose of whatever effect(s) you're using.

INSERT
This will most commonly be a channel insert, so the processor works on just one signal, but you might conceivably use a group insert, where all the signals on that group will be processed.

AUX/EFFECT SENDS AND RETURNS
This probably seems the most obvious way to use effects, with the attraction that you can vary how much effect each channel's signal receives. The drawback is that you'll be tying up a whole effect send if you want the effect on only one channel.

TAPE/TRACK OUT
This is mainly applicable to multi-track cassette machines, which generally have direct track outputs. You take the signal from the appropriate track output to the processor, then feed its output back into one of the machine's

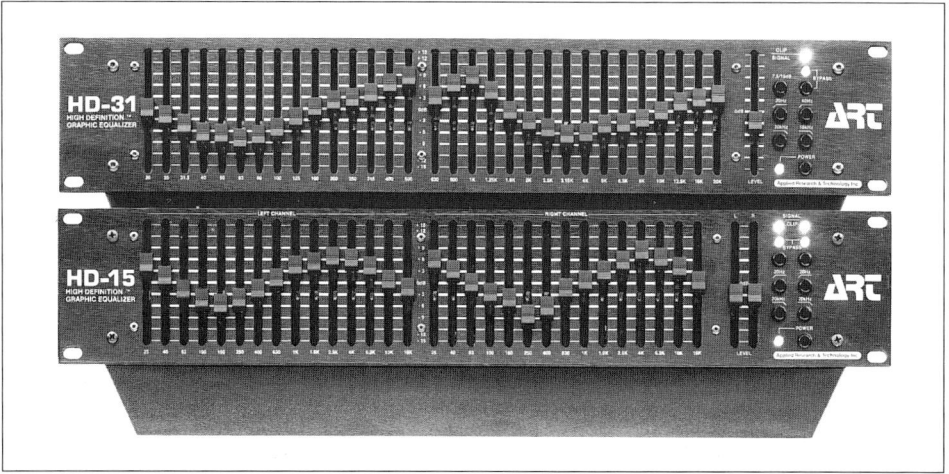

Graphic EQ is useful for overall tone-shaping; parametric is best for highly specific EQ

inputs (usually the same-numbered channel as the track involved, but not necessarily). You could use the same method with a separate mixer/recorder setup, by inserting the processor in the tape-to-mixer connection.

With so many options, the obvious question is: which to use when? Fortunately, the answer is usually quite straightforward, simply by considering how you want an effect to operate. If you want the effect on all signals equally, then out-line is by far the simplest, but as I mentioned above, you need a stereo processor. If you want the effect on several signals but in differing amounts, then an aux/effect send is the solution. In-line, insert and track out methods are ideal for effects on single channels, but in-line means you'll be recording 'wet' (see below), unless the source is a virtual track.

The terms 'dry' and 'wet' simply distinguish between the 'raw' un-effected signal, and the same signal after it has received its dose of effect processing. With the exceptions of lo-cut filtering to remove pops and ambient background 'rumble', and the use of moderate compression on vocals, the ideal is almost always to record dry, simply because this keeps all your options open until mixdown time, when you can judge an effect in the context of the overall mix. Unfortunately, as discussed in *Engineering And Production*, this isn't always practical, with your need for effects potentially far exceeding the number of available processors.

EQ

Fixed, sweep, parametric and graphic EQ can all be powerful tools, but like most powerful things, they need using with care. The main point is that what sounds impressive for just a few seconds, or when an instrument is played on its own, may well be too strong in the final mix.

With regard to sweep EQ, I've often read the snappy little slogan 'park it and peak it', which means that you first set the frequency range, then apply the boost or cut. I have to say that I regard this as crazy – how can you set the frequency range if there's no boost or cut to enable you to hear what the effect will be? The more practical approach can be summarised as 'peak, sweep, and tweak' – first set some boost or cut (maybe halfway to the full setting), then sweep to find the frequency range you want to work on, and finally tweak the boost/cut. Parametric isn't quite so easy, but the Q/width control is best set roughly at the same time as the sweep, then tweaked along with the boost/cut. Graphic is useful for gentle overall 'tone-shaping', but usually inferior to parametric for highly-specific EQ, not least because it can take a lot longer to get the settings the way you want them.

Two practical points: many people tend to use EQ 'additively', which means that they boost the frequencies they want to be more prominent – if you find you're doing this over large parts of the frequency range, you might consider replacing the boost with cut at the frequencies you want to be less prominent. Also, though the idea of EQ in/out switches for wet/dry comparisons may seem attractive, the EQed signal is going to be louder or quieter (depending on whether you're boosting or cutting) than the dry signal, and it's a well-known fact that a louder signal generally tends to sound more impressive – you may need to adjust the channel level to allow for this.

REVERB

Even the most basic modern reverb will have at least three controls: input level, program select, and mix. The input control will have some kind of level indicator, and as with all things digital, it's essential that you don't go into the red – this tends to happen as you add more channels to the reverb send, and means that it's a good idea to set up the reverb unit where the overload LED will catch your eye.

Choosing a program can be a time-consuming process – the more programs on offer, the longer it can take to work through them. This can

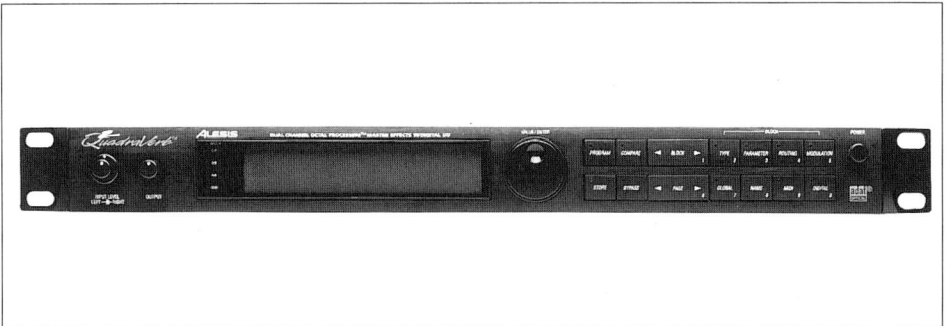

The more reverb programs on offer, the longer it can take to find the one you really want

become a serious problem if you're using two or more reverbs to create different 'layers' of depth. The best approach is to plough through the programs sometime when you're not doing any serious recording, and make a note of those you like – this is vastly preferable to interrupting proceedings when you're on a creative roll. If you're using multiple reverbs, you'll generally find that you can maximise the impression of depth by using relatively bright programs for upfront elements, and softer/warmer ones for sources you want to place further away. Some programs create what are called 'early reflections', which are like 'mini-echoes' before the reverb proper gets going. These can be Bad News on percussive instruments, for example, by making it sound like each cymbal stroke has been played twice.

The final control on a basic reverb will be labelled 'mix', and this simply sets the balance between dry and wet signals. If you're using the reverb with an effect send and return, you'll set the mix to fully-wet, then vary the dry/wet balance using the effect return level control. However you create this mix, it can be used in conjunction with your choice of program – you could use a small room program with a very wet mix, or a large hall program (which would be far too reverberant and 'muddy' on its own) with a much drier balance.

Note that though you'll probably use an effect send to drive the reverb when doing a 'proper' mix, you may also want reverb on the foldback during track-laying, and in many cases it will be easiest to do this by connecting the reverb between monitor output and amplifier. This means you won't be able to use the mixer/recorder's own phones output, but the advantages of using the main monitor amp are that it will probably give more volume, and that the mere act of plugging in your phones will reduce the risk of feedback/howlround blowing up your speakers.

COMPRESSORS

Compressors can feature all sorts of controls to tweak their operation, but the four most common are the compression ratio itself, plus threshold, attack and release.

The two main uses of a compressor are with vocals, and on the overall final mix. For vocals, the exact compression ratio depends both on the vocalist's style, and on how you want to present the voice in the mix – ballparking wildly, you're probably looking at something between 3:1 and 8:1. Overall mix compression is often influenced by the kind of music you're making – acoustic folk might have little or none, while thrash metal will usually use quite heavy compression. If you're going to have both vocal and overall compression, with the former being applied during track-laying, bear in mind that it's going to get an extra dose later, which means using rather less initial compression than you actually want to end up with.

Threshold is a very important control because, if you think of, say, a

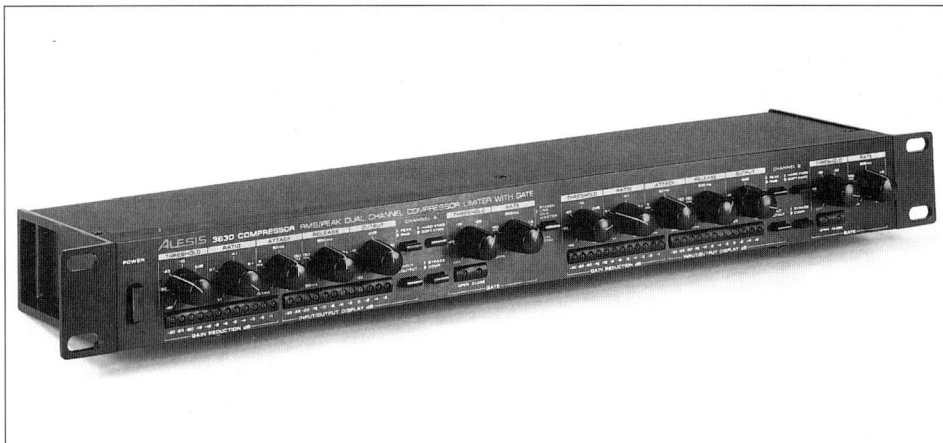

The two main uses of a compressor are with vocals, and on the overall final mix

4:1 compression ratio on a signal that has a natural dynamic range of 60dB, you're compressing this into just 15dB, the implication of which is that you're bringing the 'noise-floor' up from 60dB below peak to just 15dB below, and this may well make whatever gunge is in the noise unpleasantly obvious. The threshold control partly overcomes this, by leaving all signals below your chosen threshold level setting uncompressed.

Attack and release determine the time aspects of a compressor's operation. Attack sets how soon the compressor will start acting after a signal peak exceeds the threshold, while release controls how long the compression will continue after the signal drops below the threshold. Too fast an attack kills natural dynamics, and actually alters the sound of instruments, while too fast a release produces nasty 'pumping' or 'breathing' effects on material with rapid dynamics, such as a drum kit. Start with these controls in their centre positions, and only mess with them when things sound wrong.

NOISE GATES

The three basic controls are threshold, delay and rate. Threshold determines the signal level at which the gate will open and close – set it too high and you'll lose the end of every note; set it too low and you'll get some of the background noise after every note. The easiest way of setting the threshold is to find these two points, then simply set the control to halfway between them.

Delay is the equivalent of a compressor's attack control, while rate determines the speed at which the gate closes – at one extreme the gate is 'slammed' shut (sudden cut-off); at the other it closes gradually, giving a brief fade-out. Fairly typically, you'd opt for a long delay and slow rate on vocals, but a short delay and fast rate on snare drum.

An enhancer is intended for making one or two elements stand out in a mix

ENHANCERS

Using an enhancer is a delicate art, partly because, as with any effect, it's easy to overdo things, but probably more often because, once you get into the results an enhancer can create, it's tempting to use it on everything. The point to remember here is that the whole purpose of an enhancer (except when restoring lost treble) is to make just one, or maybe two, elements stand out in a mix. If you use it on everything, you may well create an exciting sound (ho, ho), but you won't get the stand-out effect.

Enhancer controls vary quite considerably, both in what they do and what they're called, but the most common and important are likely to be labelled 'bandwidth' and 'mix'/'balance'. Bandwidth determines the lowest frequency at which the enhancer starts generating its extra treble, while mix/balance acts just as on a reverb, controlling how much of the new treble gets into the final signal. For vocals, you'd probably keep the bandwidth up towards the high end, and at the other extreme, you'd set it relatively low into the mid-band to emphasise the breathy quality on a sax.

MIXING

A good mix can enhance even the finest raw material but it won't hide a dodgy cardigan

Mixing can be part of almost any stage of the recording process, from bringing several mikes together to create stereo drums, or mixing DIed and miked guitar, through track bouncing, and on to the final mixdown to stereo. While even the best mixing can't rescue a putrid performance, a good mix can equally definitely enhance even the finest raw material. When we get down to brass tacks, most mixing decisions are basically about production values, and what I want to do in this chapter is look at some general aspects of planning and constructing mixes, along with a few specific techniques.

THE SOUNDSTAGE

There's a lot more to this than just the concept of stereo placement – for example, anyone remember the old Motown/Phil Spector 'wall of sound'? This was very much about soundstaging, even though most listeners heard the results in mono.

The most obvious point here is about how the instruments you choose, and the way you mix them, occupy the frequency range from deep bass through to high treble. Many choices in this area are primarily musical, but it's useful to plan with the final mix in mind. One of the main ideas here is to avoid 'conflict' (which is where two musical elements compete for the listener's attention, rather than complementing one another). You might get this with two 'middy' keyboard voices playing at the same time. More subtle cases include slap bass together with a 'smacky' bass drum. The high ends of both occupy the same frequency range; this is fine if you're going to have them create a complex rhythm by 'playing off' each other, but it could be a Right Sod when you want them to play on exactly the same beat – any timing slackness will be gruesomely highlighted.

Another aspect of timing is the actual duration of notes/sounds, and their 'internal textures/dynamics'. As with frequency, there's a range involved – taking the extremes, you could have a single bass note that lasts throughout an entire track (almost certainly disastrous), through to a note that's so short you literally don't notice it. Again, this is primarily musical territory, but it's useful to know that, in soundstage terms, you could have two instruments covering the same frequency range, but avoid conflict by having dramatically different durations, textures or dynamics. This could apply to the 'middy' keyboard voices mentioned above, or to take a recent commercial example, the 'creamy' bass pad alongside the 'tight' bass drum on "Streets of Philadelphia".

OK, time for the stereo side of soundstaging. Many people think of stereo as meaning two channels, but these two channels are merely the means to an end, and we find that end in the original Greek meaning of 'stereo' – solid. What we're talking about here is three-dimensional sound, as in left-right, front-back, and even up-down. This last is seldom exploited in mainstream commercial recordings, and most of these also keep the left-right dimension to within the boundaries set by the speakers, while front-back effects are commonly created by a combination of level, reverb and (maybe) miking distance. All this may seem obvious, but I think it's worth spelling things out, because the arrival of 3-D effects (such as Roland's Sound Space series) is beginning to open-up major possibilities beyond the conventional stereo soundstage. It remains to be seen how they're used, and how listeners like the results.

Even within conventional stereo, there's quite a lot to consider. If there's a possibility your production will be cut to vinyl, there are technical reasons why you should keep any really deep bass in the centre of the stage. Even with cassette and CD, a centre position may make sense for bass – it's at low frequencies that most speakers have to work hardest, and if your bass line is 'strong', it makes sense to share the workload between both speakers.

Lead vocals also usually go centre-stage. There's no technical reason for this, so you might want to try being different. Personally, I don't recommend it, because if you listen to many early Sixties recordings where they played about with this, it certainly sounds different, but it equally certainly sounds wrong. If there are two lead vocals, you'll probably want to separate them, and you should be able to achieve this sufficiently by panning one to ten o'clock and the other to two o'clock.

Even when you do want an instrument to go far-left or far-right, there are a couple of reasons why you should resist pushing the pan control all the way to the end-stop. The major consideration is what's called 'mono compatibility', and the problem is that anything panned to extreme left or right will suffer a level change when listened to in mono (which in turn screws up the mix balance). The more subtle point, for stereo listeners, is that you're probably adding reverb. To be convincing, this should extend beyond the sound source; if the source is, say, hard-left, the reverb can only extend to the right of it. The solution to both problems is simple: you'll get ample stereo width and separation if you treat far-left as eight o'clock on the pan control, and far-right as four o'clock (as distinct from the extremes of seven o'clock and five o'clock – on a typically-labelled pan, one 'tick' short of maximum). Note that you can safely pan hard-over with the two channels of *stereo* sources (like a pre-mixed drum kit), because there will already be some spillage/leakage between the channels.

The convincing portrayal of depth is quite different from just saying, "I want this to be quiet in the mix." Level is certainly the starting point, but we can use effects, most notably reverb, to enhance the depth element. If you're stuck with just a single reverb, you can't do much more than put extra reverb on sounds you want to be well back; with multiple reverbs you could use a 'bright' program for upfront stuff, and a softer one for elements you want to be further back. Note that this needn't affect your choice of actual reverb times – you'll often find you can mess with these, and even echo, without necessarily upsetting the depth perceptions created by the tonal character of the reverbs.

PRACTICAL MIXING

First, let's consider the basics of building a mix. Most people start with drums, but this is only really necessary if you've got them spread over several tracks, in which case you'll want to create their 'internal' balance first, and, ideally, assign the result to a group-pair, so you can adjust overall drum level without disturbing the individual channels/tracks. Now's the time to get any drum-specific effects (such as snare gating) into action, while over at the stereo end of proceedings, you want a peak level of around -6dB. Next comes

Keeping a note of all the mixer and effect settings is vital when trying different mixes

bass, be it guitar and/or keyboard, normally followed by vocals, then rhythm stuff, lead guitar(s), keyboards, brass and such, and backing vocals. As you're setting the levels, switch between stereo and mono.

Time to start playing seriously with effects, and there are two extremes of approach here. One is, 'If it ain't broke, don't fix it'; the other is, 'Explore every possibility'. (If you like: 'Effects: tweak 'em or freak 'em.') Both are equally valid, though a great deal of modern music is produced using the latter philosophy (a far cry from the old saying: 'effects should be noticed by their absence, not their presence').

You may find that the best way of creating effects on individual tracks is to listen to the overall mix for ideas, switch to solo to actually set the effect(s) you want, then back to the main mix to assess the result. For a lot of people, particularly when they're fairly new to recording, this mix-to-solo-to-mix lark can seem to go on interminably. So take heart from the fact that it's just like learning to play an instrument: the first few times you want a new chord, you have to really work at it, but after a while you just think, 'I want that chord', and there it is. What makes life particularly difficult with effects is that what sounds right in the mix may sound totally weird when soloed. There is, of course, nothing to stop you creating a track's effects while listening to the mix (and that's what you'll be pretty much forced to do if your mixer doesn't have solo).

Throughout both basic level mixing and adding effects, you should be switching between main and mini-monitors every step of the way. Depending on your set-up, if it sounds wrong on both, then it very probably *is* wrong; if it sounds wrong on just one, then think of it like an amber traffic light – a warning. Try listening at different volumes, but bear in mind that it takes our ears and brains a couple of minutes to adjust from really high to low volumes. Some people recommend getting an overall impression of a mix by trying things like listening from outside the room; alternatively, simply to talk over the mix and, ideally, have someone talk back to you – this can be a very good guide to what aspects of the music and mix will stand out in 'normal' listening situations.

In an ideally simple world, you'd get the mix you want, record it to your stereo deck, and still have time to knock up a completely original arrangement of "Stairway". But in reality... Well, for a start, there's the classic 'band problem', where each member wants a different mix. The idea of working out a compromise isn't necessarily too hot, because it's easy to end up trying not to offend anyone, which in turn leads towards concepts like 'bland'. In this situation, I recommend letting everyone and their dog have a bash at constructing a mix, record the results, and play them to all your friends who are into your music. This kind of thing clearly takes time, especially since you really need to make a note of all the mixer and effect settings for each mix, in order to be able to recreate them later.

This point about keeping notes is also relevant to solo artists – if you don't, what you gonna do when a record label likes your demo cassette so much, they phone up and say, "Don't change a thing, just master it to DAT"?

Some 'hands-on' stuff: you may often find that levels need changing at various points within a track – the classic case is lead guitar, which may need taking down a few dBs every time the vocals enter, then up again for riffs between lyric lines and for solos. This kind of fun is known as 'ducking', 'cos you're 'ducking' one signal under another. You can get automatic duckers, and it's a feature on some compressors (equally, one can argue that the guitarist should have built the level changes into his playing in the first place). Still, if you need to do it by hand, you may find it quite tricky to combine moving the fader both quickly and accurately. A Crafty Dodge here is to use two blobs of BluTack, one above and the other below the fader, their exact positions respectively setting the 'full' and 'ducked' levels; you can then whang the fader between the two with totally predictable and repeatable results.

Ducking is actually a special case of a more general mixing game: 'gain-riding'. As a hypothetical example, let's say you've got a drum loop, and you want alternate snare beats to come out extra-loud. You could program this, but you can give it a more 'human' feel by doing it manually – as with ducking, you might find BluTack helpful. There may also be situations where you want much slower gain-riding, such as gradually building an instrument's 'presence' throughout an entire track.

This opens the door to the whole subject of musical dynamics, the finer points of which are well outside the scope of this book. But what's important from the mixing angle is that, by definition, dynamics require that some bits be louder than others. The most common example is that old reviewer's cliché, 'the music gradually built to a climax', which in turn means that it started off rather more quietly. The obvious problem is that a quiet start is usually the very last thing you want, simply because it will almost certainly fail to grab the listeners' attention. One solution is to start the track with a musical 'bang', then quieten things down for a while – listen to the heavy drums and electric guitar intro on "Love Is All Around", which is followed by the much quieter acoustic guitar and vocal.

The other main occasion when you need some form of 'dynamics management' is when extra instruments are added as a track progresses – again, you probably want to avoid the 'start quiet, end loud' syndrome, and what this means in practice is that, as the additional instruments enter, you actually need to slightly reduce the levels of at least some of the other components. This has to be done with considerable subtlety, so listeners don't notice the manipulation, and actually think that overall levels are building up, even though they're not. You can confirm this for yourself, by watching the levels throughout many commercial tracks – subjectively, the loudest part may indeed be the end, but the meters will often show that peak levels are in fact pretty constant throughout the whole song.

Which brings us to the end of the track. By convention, fades usually start at the beginning of a bar, and finish at the end of one – you'll very possibly need to practise a few times to judge it right. Left to itself, a fade can easily be boring – if you've only got a few tracks, or your desk has sufficient groups, you can make proceedings more interesting by fading different elements at different rates – a totally-unoriginal example would be a fairly fast fade on lead guitar, and a relatively slower one on drums and bass.

Beware of really long, slow fades – these can work (as on several tracks from 'On Every Street'), but they can also go horribly wrong (try Brian Ferry's version of 'Jealous Guy'). Such fades may sound fine at high levels, but are at their worst when music is playing as a backdrop to conversation. Play 'Jealous Guy' in these circumstances, and I can pretty much guarantee you'll end up looking over at the hi-fi to see why the music's stopped. If you do want a slow fade, the trick is to start it off at a 'normal' pace for the first 2–3dB (so that listeners realise they're into fadesville), then slow it way, way down for most of the rest of the duration, finally going from what should still be a moderate volume to the end quite quickly. Try it.

On tracks with a 'proper' ending, it's generally worth taking the master(s) down as the last note ends – there's almost always some background noise, be it from miked background 'mush', tape, mixer or effects, and this is less noticeable if it's faded out over maybe a second, rather than being suddenly chopped-off.

TRACK BOUNCING

We talked about this way back in *A Quick Tour* (where I said that the major problem is putting together a bounce mix that will still sound right when you've added all the later tracks), and in *Engineering & Production* (where I suggested trying to plan bounces so that they involve elements that tend to 'group' together naturally, like drums, bass and rhythm).

There's one stunt that can help check and fine-tune bounce mixes, but it's fairly time-consuming: put together your best guess at the mix, and record it onto your stereo deck, then copy this back to a new multi-track tape. You can then try adding further parts on the other tracks, and see how the bounce balance holds up. There are a couple of points to note if you do this. If your stereo recorder is digital (DAT), the multi-to-stereo-to-multi sound quality loss will hopefully be only slightly greater than that involved in an ordinary bounce.

So if the bounce balance holds up, and you just happen to deliver a 'once in a lifetime' performance while trying out a new track, you can keep both it and the bounce mix, and just forget the original multi-track tape. Also, if your DAT has timecode, you could sync it with the multitrack, so now if you get that brilliant performance, but don't like the bounce mix, you can go back to the original multitrack, remix and DAT it, then copy it back over the bounce track(s) on the new tape. Clever stuff.

MIDI, SYNC & COMPUTERS

The Musical Instrument Digital Interface (also known as the Maddeningly Intricate Digital Interface) is as important to modern music as multi-track, digital and, of course, computers themselves. MIDI works like a language, enabling musical instruments to 'talk' to each other and to other devices.

One of MIDI's great strengths is that you, the user, can exploit as

Since the mid-eighties, more and more home recordists have exploited MIDI sequencing

Alesis present the dream MIDI studio – not an acoustic instrument or vocalist in sight

little or as much of its potential as suits your needs. A full-blown MIDI set-up might include the following: a 'master' keyboard controlling just about any number of synth modules, an analogue or digital multi-track, automated mixing, samplers, effects, and a sequencer program running the whole caboodle from a PC, Macintosh or the like.

Since the mid-eighties, more and more home recordists have exploited MIDI sequencing. A sequencer can record musical performances and play them back via your MIDI instruments. It can be a hardware device (either a separate stand-alone unit or one built-in to a 'workstation' or other keyboard or module), or it can take the form of sequencing software running on a desktop computer. The sequencer records performance details, not audio information, and therefore offers some particular advantages over tape recording. Mistakes can be corrected without the need to re-record, tempo may be adjusted without affecting pitch (so difficult passages may be recorded slowly), and changes to the song structure can be made simply and easily – without razor blades or splicing tape.

This is clearly a vast subject, and one with many complications. For a thorough general grounding in MIDI, there's the *Making Music* handbook *What's MIDI?'* – though for the ins and outs (a weak MIDI joke) of getting specific hardware and software to work together you really need an experienced retailer, plus manufacturer/importer back-up.

The two aspects of MIDI I want to consider here are sequencing and syncing. A sequencer is basically a fairly straightforward device – you tell it what you want played and when, it stores the info, then tells the keyboard or whatever to do the right thing at the right time. Many modern keyboards (and all those with the buzzword 'workstation') have an on-board sequencer, though the majority are let down by fairly rudimentary editing facilities, and the limitations of communicating through a small LCD screen.

The big step up in sequencing is to move the job away from the music-producing components, and onto an out-board computer. Such a computer is commonly called a 'platform', and could be anything from a £90 Commodore 64, through a basic PC at maybe £500, up to a £4000+ PC or Macintosh. On top of the hardware price, the sequencing software itself could cost anything from £30 to £300+. On mid- to top-price products, look for established names like **Steinberg** (best known for **Cubase**), **Emagic**, **Mark**

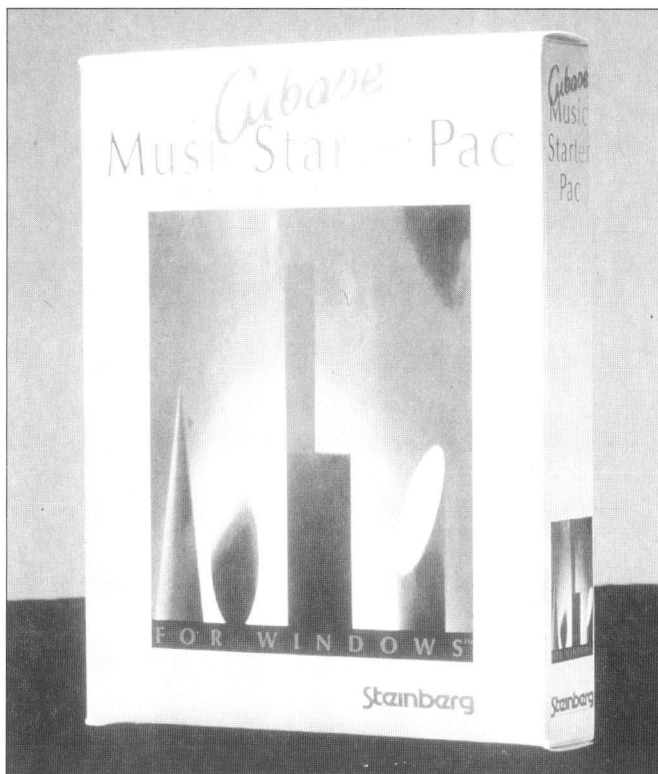

Cubase: one of the most popular sequencing programs

of the Unicorn, **Opcode** and **Passpor**t. These are the guys who are most likely to be there when you need after-sales support (and believe me, you may well need it).

With price ranges like this, you'd expect there to be big performance differences, and there are. Some of these are obvious, such as the number of sequencing 'tracks' and the presentation of the 'user interface'. Others only become apparent with extended use. The most widely-accepted general advice is to pick your software first, then choose the hardware to suit; this is not as helpful as it used to be, when many software products were only available for this or that machine, and today you may have a choice of platforms to run the same software (though usually with slight differences in, at least, the user interface).

For some music and music-making styles, a sequencer, along with its sequenced instruments, is all you need. But very often, musos want to mix sequenced 'virtual' tracks with 'real' tracks, most typically vocals, guitar and drums. If these are being recorded on tape, you need some way to 'lock' the tape and sequencer together, so everything happens in time. Enter synchronisation – commonly abbreviated to 'sync'.

The obvious idea for sync is simply to record MIDI timing signals on the tape, then use them on playback to control the timing of everything else. Unfortunately, MIDI information is not in a form that can be recorded directly to analogue tape, so we need a gizmo called a MIDI-FSK converter (otherwise known simply as a synchroniser). FSK stands for frequency shift keying, and is a term from radio telecommunications of about 50 years ago – digital noughts and ones become two different and easily-recorded frequencies, but the resulting sound equally easily crosstalks or leaks onto the adjacent tape track.

All current multi-tracks support sync, though dbx machines need a switch to be set for the track in use. Unlike audio signals, where you optimise the record level by taking it as high as possible, you aim to minimise sync crosstalk by keeping the level as low as possible, while still getting reliable 'lock-up' with the sequencer. As a very general guide, you should hope to get away with a level of -10 dB or slightly lower.

On the very simplest MIDI gear, the timing info may be just the MIDI equivalent of a metronome click. If you rewind the tape to a mid-track point, things go haywire, because the sequencer doesn't know where it's up to. Most modern gear overcomes this by providing 'song position pointer' data to be recorded on the tape, while MTC (MIDI time code) is even better. These facilities enable the provision of 'chase 'n' lock', which is where you start the tape mid-track, and the sequencer recognises where the tape is, and 'chases' or rushes through its stored sequence, until it reaches the required point, then 'locks' with the tape. A more refined version is where the tape recorder itself is under MIDI control using MMC (MIDI machine control), and you can tell the sequencer to start at a certain point, with the tape then fast-winding to reach that point.

The chase 'n' lock process not only takes time, but even when the required point is reached, there's a delay while all the various bits get up to speed and in-sync. This brings in the concept of 'pre-roll', which is where the system starts running before the required point, in the (sometimes vain) hope that everything will come together by the desired point. Pre-roll times are usually variable up to ten seconds or more, which gives you some idea of the 'drag' time you might have to endure (even a more typical five seconds can seem like an eternity if you're kicking your heels at 140bpm).

MIDI-FSK converters typically cost around £150, so if all you want to do is sync a drum box to a multi-track, it makes mucho sense to buy a drum box with an onboard converter.

Computers have musical applications beyond sequencing, which uses very little of any decent computer's processing power and memory. The most attractive concept is to combine sequencing with digital hard disk recording, sampling, and digital signal processing (DSP) such as effects, EQ and mixing. With the exception of the last two items, this recipe is very similar to the MIDI studio set-up I described earlier, the important difference being that in this case, everything takes place in one box, instead of a room-full of gear connected by miles of audio and MIDI cables.

Doing all of these things simultaneously is well beyond the abilities of the average personal computer, so you need all sorts of add-ons to handle the nitty-gritty: ADCs and DACs (analogue-to-digital and digital-to analogue converters), DSPs, plus of course, a big fast hard-disk for recording, oodles (maybe 16megabytes) of memory for samples, and the software to run everything. Most systems are eight- or 16-track, but some allow for expansion (usually requiring one or more extra disk drives, as opposed to just one larger drive). As with stand-alone hard disk recorders, there may be restrictions on the number of tracks you can record at once, and also on the number of audio outputs. In what I regard as a good move, some manufacturers are bringing out products where both these aspects are upgradeable. Major names include **Cubase** (for Atari and Mac), **DigiDesign** (PC and Mac), **Software Audio Workshop** (PC), and **Soundscape** (PC).

As a very rough ballpark, a complete system might cost four grand on a PC, a little more on a Mac, and rather less on an Atari Falcon. The Falcon may win on price, but it's a new machine, so there isn't the wide range of add-on and software options that are available for the other two; also, I hear reports that the Falcon's DSP sound quality may not be up to true pro standards. On the other hand, it's precisely because of the vast variety of options, that choosing a Mac or, even worse, a PC, can be complicated. If you're confused or unsure, speak to a specialist dealer who can translate your needs (both current and with regard to upgrade options) into the hard 'n' software that will do the job. No single dealer will be offering the lowest price on every item you need, so this approach will probably cost you more (maybe ten to 15 percent) than shopping round for the best price on each component. But if such an idea appeals, you might like to bear in mind that a single month's issue of *Personal Computer World* currently runs over 600 pages – that's a lot of ads to sift through. There's also the more-than-marginally vital point that if you buy from several sources, and problems develop, you may well become an unwilling connoisseur of the art of 'buck-passing'.

Computer technology is changing faster than any other area of music making and recording, and what is state of the art today will almost certainly be end-of-line bargain basement within, say, three years. This doesn't really matter though, because if you can afford the kit at today's prices, it should still be delivering the goods in three years' time.

LIVE RECORDING

A regular venue will attract your keenest fans and encourage your best performances

There are several reasons for wanting to record your live performances: to assess your music-making, as a demo (particularly for venue managers and promoters), and as an actual product to sell to your fans.

If you only want to hear how well/badly you played, you can keep the recording side really simple – lots of bands get along with just a mike-equipped radio-cassette. The main problem with this is likely to be that the mike position picks up a musically unbalanced result; a single PZM taped to the floor directly in front of the lead vocalist will often be an improvement, while a pair on the side-walls can be used for stereo (possibly have them behind the vocal PA if the drums aren't loud enough).

At the other extreme, it's possible that you've reached the stage where everything is already miked or DIed into a main PA. This gives you two fairly simple options: record the PA mix direct to stereo, or send each channel to its own recorder track. The former has the attraction of cheapness, but there are also a couple of pitfalls – the PA mix may well be balanced and EQed to suit the PA speakers, the level of the amps on stage, and the venue acoustics; also the balance itself may be pretty ropey if you don't have an out-front mixing engineer (this may not bother the audience too much, because they can see what's going on, but it could sound awful on playback). As for the channels-to-tracks idea, well, this is fine – provided you just happen to have a 16-track handy, or you're prepared to hire one.

Most semi-pro live recording lies somewhere between simple PZM and top-end channels-to-tracks, but there are so many variations in both band line-up and recording facilities that it's only possible to give the most general guidelines. To iIllustrate the fact that the principal problems are usually insufficient inputs, busses and tracks, let's consider a situation: drums, bass and lead guitars, keyboards, lead and backing vocals – all having to cram onto a four-track. The worst case is clearly a Porta with only two-track record, where you have to record in stereo; even so, it's unlikely such a machine will have enough inputs for every instrument, so you're effectively back to just a couple of PZMs.

Things are a little brighter with four-track record and six inputs. Probably the most sensible approach is to choose the two most important musical elements (the two you really need to be able to control at mixdown), and give each of these its own track, using the remaining tracks for a stereo mix of everything else. The two 'key' elements will usually be lead vocals and drums, and straight away we're in trouble – the lead singer's mike almost certainly goes into a PA along with backing vocals, so you have to take the vocals as a whole from the DI out. (It's no use using a splitter cable or channel-out to bring the lead vocals independently to the recorder, because you can't then get the backing vocals without the lead – unless the PA mixer has a spare aux send.) Drums can only have a single (overhead) mike, because the stereo buss will be busy with the two-track mix, so there's no buss to mix two mikes onto one track. (You could mix them onto a spare aux send, but you'd then need another direct-to-track input to bring the aux mix to tape).

Eight-track cassette recorders may have more inputs, but they can still only record on four tracks at once. An eight-track 'separates' system should be OK, provided you've got enough groups to do several stereo pre-mixes.

The really wretched thing about any live recording (short of the full-blown channels-to-tracks), is that you have to do a certain amount of mixing at the recording stage, and since you can't mix without the band playing, there will be so much noise that even listening on closed-back cans won't tell you much about the mix you're constructing. There's also the little problem of how you combine mixing and playing at the same time. Fortunately, where there's a will there's also a regular venue.

Almost every semi-pro gigging band finds at least one place where their music goes down particularly well, and which becomes a regular. For all sorts of reasons, this is the place to do your live recording. From the mixing aspect, you can record a rough 'n' ready production first time round, and then, provided you make a note of all the control settings, playback should give you a good idea of how to refine things for the next time you're there. This also gives you the chance to experiment with mike placement.

There's more good news: a regular venue will attract your keenest fans, and their enthusiasm will often encourage you to produce your best performances; also, if you're making a demo for a venue manager or promoter, audience appreciation is the single most important aspect of your tape – it confirms that you can draw a (money-spending) crowd, which is, down on the bottom-line, the only reason for these guys wanting to book you. (Taking this a couple of steps further, make sure the lead vocalist holds his mike out to the audience at the end of each number, which both ensures good pick-up and hopefully encourages the audience to clap/shout/scream even louder. Also, when you produce your final demo mix, it's fine to have the audience really loud, but don't let it go on for too long – profit-conscious venue managers know that a screaming fan cannot simultaneously be a drink-buying fan...)

A few practical points. Whether you're using cassettes, open-reel or ADAT (as distinct from DAT or Hi-8), you'll need someone to change tapes; with cassettes, pre-wind the replacements so they're past the leader and ready to go. Keep the record levels well down – if you're setting them during a sound check, don't let the peaks go above -3 dB (-12 for digital), and even then, cut them back still further at the interval (bands almost always play louder in the second set).

Finally, and Very Importantly, only power your recording gear from the same mains socket(s) that are running your instruments, backline and PA. Lots of public buildings get their mains supply in what's called 'three-phase' form – without getting techno, the point is that two sockets, even though only a few feet apart, can be on 'separate phases', which in turn means that when you connect an audio lead between two thingies running off different sockets, both items get a Right Wallop (like 415V at maybe 50A). Explosions and fires can be fascinating things to watch, but seldom when it's your own gear that's providing the pyrotechnics. You Have Been Warned...

COPYING & DUPLICATING

There are many variations on the theme of copying and duplicating – you might want just a few cassettes for your friends, or maybe a few dozen for demos, or even a few hundred to sell at gigs. Then again, you might want just a one-off CD to use for backing tracks at gigs, or as many as 500 if you're 'self-releasing' on your own label. And then there's vinyl...

With cassettes, the basic question is whether to DIY or go to a commercial duplicator. DIY is almost always the answer if you're just knocking out a few tapes for fun, while commercial copying is equally often the preferred route if you want several hundred. But the situation in-between these two extremes is much less clear.

There are really three factors to consider: sound quality, visual image, and price. The first aspect of sound quality is the result you're likely to achieve if you DIY. The twin cassette decks in most midi systems are truly abysmal, the most common problems being seriously bad wow and flutter (the old 'drunkeness' and 'gargling' nasties), and near-total destruction of the music's dynamics due to the action of the recorders' ALC (automatic level control) circuits. And if you try to speed up the copying by using the high-speed option, you'll wipe out most of the treble. The twin decks sold for use in separates systems usually have manual level control, but their overall sound quality is generally well short of the standard you'd get by spending the same money on two single decks.

By the time you get as far as, say, a couple of budget Aiwas (or a DAT plus cassette), you'll potentially be getting results that are pretty much on a par with a decent commercial duplicator, and you can avoid the end-product looking home-made by using custom-wound cassettes and a computer printer for labels and inlay cards. But hold on, what about that word 'potentially'? Well, the fact is that many musos end up using a commercial duplicator, simply because the results sound better. Given that your copying gear is of a reasonable standard, the cause of this strange situation is that, between your master tape and the finished product, there is a stage called post-production.

There are many aspects to post-production, but what we're interested in here is that it provides a last opportunity to 'sweeten' your master tape. This might be desirable if your monitoring gear has caused you to produce a weird tonal balance, but it can also allow for quality losses that

A couple of budget Aiwas will give quality comparable to a professional duping house

will occur in the duplicating process (for example, by upping the extreme treble). Post-production is essential if you're going to vinyl or CD – for vinyl your master will need EQ and probably some compression, while for CD, there are all sorts of time-codes to be put on the final master tape.

If you want the very cheapest price, you'll probably do best to negotiate duplicating and printing separately, but to my mind there's a lot to be said for the 'one-stop' service that many companies provide – if nothing else, it means there's only one person for you to hassle. The majority of these companies also offer artwork origination, which is fine for relatively simple stuff, but given that we're talking about a price-competitive industry, you can't really expect a professional artist to devote a week to conjuring up a total image for you (see *Demos*).

COMMERCIAL STUDIOS

You probably wouldn't be reading this book if you were going to do all your recording in a commercial studio, and I certainly wouldn't be writing it if there weren't many thousands of musos who would rather work in their own studio at home. But although home recording continues to become ever more popular (and to represent an ever higher percentage of commercial releases), the pro studio does still have its place.

Some good reasons for at least considering using a commercial studio include: quieter and/or better acoustics for miked work, more facilities for recording a whole band in a single take, more and (maybe) better effects, a range of instruments, and the services of an engineer. Also, depending on your own and the studio's gear, you should expect better overall sound quality. And though one of the beauties of working at home is that there shouldn't be any time pressure, not all home environments are conducive to concentrated work (interruptions by family/telephone/Jehovah's Witnesses...) – in this respect a pro studio can be like a 'retreat'.

But there are reasons why using a studio may not be attractive, and by far the biggest is cost. Fairly obviously, there are two elements here: the basic cost per hour (which is often just a starting point for negotiations), and the much more difficult subject of how many hours/days/decades you'll actually need.

Studio costs per hour vary wildly, partly according to facilities, but also influenced by location, local competition, and reputation/trendiness. At the very bottom end of the market, it's only a couple of years since a local eight-track studio was cheerfully charging just £4 an hour (which is possibly why they went bust, but that's not your problem). And at the other extreme, there are studios that will equally cheerfully charge you £200 an hour, about which we will say no more.

Here in the real world, where 'real' means that it's you, not some record company, paying the bill, the most commonly-used studios are 16-track on either narrow-gauge analogue or ADAT/Hi-8 digital. As a very rough guide, analogue might cost £12-15 an hour, digital £16-20. But the real problem is, how much studio time will you need?

This is one of those 'how long is a piece of string?' questions. It depends on what you're doing, how you're doing it, how much of it you do before you get to the studio (pre-production), and how quickly you settle into

Although home recording grows ever more popular, the pro studio does have its place

working in a strange environment. Unless you're in the happy but rare position where you can afford to compose and arrange in the studio, pre-production is the single biggest key to keeping studio time under control. MIDI-based musicians can put together almost everything except any 'live' parts (such as vocals or guitar) and the final mix, initially at home, and possibly later in a MIDI pre-production studio (usually called a suite, and maybe £8 an hour), while bands can do a lot of work in rehearsal rooms (£4-ish an hour).

You probably have a fair idea of the kind of pace you work at from your home recording experience, but it would almost certainly be hopelessly optimistic to suppose you'll achieve anything like this in a studio – you might think that things would go faster with everything laid-out and to-hand, but it seldom works that way. As a very general (and very depressing) guide, many studio users find that they need about three times as long as they initially estimate. Even then, you may find you're short of time for the mixdown(s), which are notorious for taking far longer than expected. You might care to also ponder that, while a dance single may take as little as two or three days from start to finish, a complex 'live' track can easily take a week or ten days (many pros reckon on three months to do an album, which is about a track a week).

Something else that will affect your time planning is if, as with many semi-pros, band members are working weekdays and gigging nights, so the only times you can all get together for recording are Saturdays and Sundays. Each time you start a session, you can expect to waste an hour or so just getting organised (setting-up and miking instruments, rebuilding the monitor mix, and the whole psychological process of 'getting up to speed').

Very little of the above is likely to count as good news, but it's important that you face up to the possible cost before you start down the studio recording road. If you don't, you'll likely end up feeling both time *and* money pressures, with the result that the actual end-product may end up seriously compromised.

CHOOSING A STUDIO

Count yourself lucky if you live in or near London – the place is awash with studios, so not only is there a wide choice of facilities and atmosphere, but also healthy (for you) price competition. Out in the provinces, life is much more hit 'n' miss – you might have a choice of nearby studios, or there might not be any within 20 miles. Many studios advertise in the music mags, but an amazing number don't, relying entirely on word of mouth (talk to local music stores for details).

Your first move is to phone each studio, checking obvious points like number of tracks, mix automation, and basic rate, but also, and very importantly, the kind(s) of music they handle, which should act as a general guide to the sort of facilities you can expect, and the music their engineer will be familiar with. If things sound promising, fix up a time to visit.

This visit is partly about checking over what they do and don't have – depending on your needs, items like a 'live' drum booth, a 'dead' vocal booth, space for your keyboards/whatever, loads of instruments and effects for you to spend hours running up the bill playing with, and somewhere for the rest of the band to take a break while the vocalist tries for Take 87. Then there's the whole atmosphere/vibe of the place – decor, lighting, even things like temperature, humidity and stale curry smells. Is it somewhere you'd feel at least comfortable, and preferably creative?

If everything's fine, it's time to consider the one 'item' that could, more than any other, make or break your entire production... the engineer. This guy (99.5 percent of engineers are male) can bring all sorts of qualities to your production. For starters, he should be able to mike up speedily and effectively, by knowing both his microphones and the studio acoustics, and also be able to conjure up pretty much any effect you ask for at the nudge of a knob. But these are the mere mechanics of the job – what you really want is someone who is both 'sympatico' with you and your music, and able to make positive contributions, not only in terms of obvious stuff like mixing and effects, but even about musical aspects such as arrangements. In many successful studios, the engineer is just as much a kind of advisory producer as an engineer. Competence apart, this is very much person-to-person stuff, and you should spend the major part of your first visit getting to know the engineer, and sussing whether or not you can work well together. This process will be a lot easier if you take along a demo of the kind of things you're working on – if this doesn't provide you both with plenty to talk about, or if you find you're talking 'different languages', then it's time to beat a retreat.

One last check: ask the engineer to play you something he's worked on recently. This isn't necessarily a matter of, 'Do I want to sound like that?', but basic confirmation that the studio and engineer can deliver credible results, not least with regard to actual sound quality.

Finally, it's time to get down to some serious negotiating. The main subjects here are the total amount of time you want to book, and precisely when you want, or are willing, to take that time (pretty much like booking a holiday), plus of course, the little matters of when and how you're going to pay. Be sure to establish whether the prices you're talking about do or don't include VAT, and what costs extra (like tapes, floppies, overtime, and even things like instrument use and coffee). If you want to work fairly intensively (as opposed to, say, once a week), you should talk about 'lock-outs', which is where you have exclusive use of the studio, enabling you to leave instruments, mikes, mixer and effects all ready to resume from the exact point you left them at. One very important point is that, having spent a while getting to know the engineer, you insist on this same guy for your sessions – this may well affect the days and times you can book, but it's something I personally would regard as pretty much essential.

Two practical points: keep a tape running at all times – whether you're jamming or trying out a riff, you can never tell when something brill may come together, and Sod's Law decrees that if you don't have a tape rolling, you'll never be able to repeat it. Also, if you're mixing-down to cassette for your own use, be sure to record a DAT master at the same time – you just can't predict when or how this might come in handy in the future.

RECORDING COURSES

Happy students celebrate passing the 1994 diploma exams at Islington Music Workshop

There are many reasons why musicians consider signing up for recording courses, and many types of course to cater for different musos' needs.

Most musos don't actually want to become pro engineers – typically, they want enough practical tuition to make decent recordings with their own home set-up, and perhaps some knowledge of how to get the most out of using a commercial studio. Though this book is jam-packed with exactly such sound advice, it's not remotely comparable with actually having someone standing next to you saying, "Try this…" or, "No, that won't work because…" Also, even when you've absorbed all these words of wisdom, there's the old saying that 'there's a big difference between knowledge and experience'.

Hence the growing popularity of recording courses – which these days can mean anything from a one-day introduction to four-tracking, to a full-time degree or diploma in sound technology and production.

In the old days, if you wanted to learn recording, you'd have to seek an apprenticeship as a 'tape op' in a professional recording studio - basically working as a tea-boy (or, more rarely, girl), sometimes for years, before you were allowed near a mixing desk. In fact, there's still no shortage of volunteers for this kind of on-the-job training, despite the hours and conditions.

In the past decade or so, though – alongside the rapid development of home recording technology – there's been a proliferation of audio engineering courses. Costs and standards vary enormously, and not always predictably, making it impossible to give exact, representative figures. You can literally pay anything from a tenner (sometimes less) for a one-off evening class to £2500 (or even more) per year for a full-blown diploma course.

If the latter sounds out of your price range, speak to your local authority about a grant (contact your own council, not the one local to the course). If you're aged 16-19, and you want to do a BTEC NVQ (NVQs are practical, flexible courses based around job skills rather than academic theory) at a Further Education (FE) or Technology college, the council will automatically pay your fees. If you're lucky (ie poor), you might get some money to live on, too. The same goes for students of any age doing University (or other HE) degrees and HNDs.

For all other tuition (and most recording courses happen in non-state institutions, like private studios), grants and bursaries to cover fees and living costs are 'discretionary' (ie, fairly random). The best advice is to get your request in to the council early – maybe a year before the course starts – because their cash goes fast. Stress how important the course is to you, and have back-up references if possible. Beginners and hobbyists should note that community-based workshops are more likely to offer budget and concessionary rates, particularly if you're low-waged.

But what can you hope to gain from a course? You can, obviously, get plenty of recording theory and advice from excellent books like this one, so what you really need is plenty of hands-on practice. Sound recording is definitely something you learn by *doing*. Look for courses that offer the highest ratio of studio-to-classroom work, and that provide access to up-to-date technology. If your interest is mainly on the MIDI programming side, for instance, you need to be sure that this subject is adequately covered.

Apart from your tutors (usually professional engineers or producers), you may get a chance to work with new and talented musicians in a studio or live setting. The more people and styles you have to deal with, the better. And there's nothing quite like working with total strangers to concentrate your efforts. You'll also be able to make your mistakes in a controlled environment. At the end you should have an 'audio portfolio' to present to prospective employers, plus a bookful of new musical contacts.

Unfortunately, whatever the actual qualification you receive, there's

Small course groups and a friendly atmosphere make learning easier

never been any standardised accreditation of courses. Only very recently, the APRS (Association of Professional Recording Studios) set up a subsidiary Educational Members' Group, one of whose aims is to come up with a list of vetting criteria for recording courses – so there is hope that courses may soon be assessed for their practical worth.

In the meantime, try talking to some current or former students, or studio managers, for recommendations. Be warned: a lot of major studios are still wary of diploma-wielding job hunters, who may already be set in their technical ways (perhaps 'wrong' ways), or have exaggerated expectations about pay and position. One boss of a major London studio we contacted said that, in her opinion, the only thing a recording qualification proves is commitment. Even then, she makes graduates do the standard six months on the night reception desk before they're allowed on a session.

If you are thinking about sound engineering as a career, bear in mind that just as vital as the technical skills is the ability to listen and communicate; if you're not naturally suited to both of those, you're going to find studio work difficult, no matter what courses you attend. Unless it's your own studio, of course.

For a fuller discussion on the 'education in music' theme, see *Making Music*'s *Learning Special* issue, June 1994.

RECORDING COURSES: WHERE TO FIND THEM

Below is a brief and random selection of educational institutes, studios and other organisations that run recording and sound technology courses. Phone for information. *(New STD codes from April '95 in square brackets.)*

LONDON & HOME COUNTIES

Alchemea, London (071 [0171] 359 4035)
Community Music, London (071 [0171] 490 2577)
Empowerment Studios, London (081 [081] 291 5422)
Gateway School Of Recording & Music Technology, Surrey (081 [081] 549 0014)
Goldsmith's College, London (081 [081] 692 7171, ex 8000)
Greenwich Community College, London (081 [081] 519 0103)
Hope Studios, London (081 [081] 291 5422)
Islington Music Workshop, London (071 [0171] 608 0231)
Media Production Facilities, London (071 [0171] 737 7152)
Musicians' Institute, London (071 [0171] 265 0284)
Musicworks, London (071 [0171] 737 6103)
Productive Sounds, London (081 [081] 764 5401)
Queen's Park Centre, Aylesbury (0296 [01296] 24332)
School Of Audio Engineering, London (071 [0171] 609 2653)
Soundcraft, Potters Bar (0707 [01707] 665000)
University of Surrey, Guildford (0483 [01483] 509317)

THE SOUTH-WEST

Live Sound Engineering, Cornwall (0579 [01579] 62382)

THE MIDLANDS

EARTH (Electronic & Audio Research Training House), Birmingham (021 [0121] 554 7424)
Right Track Studios, Hereford (0432 [01432] 880442)
Robannas, Birmingham (021 [0121] 333 3201)

THE NORTH

City College, Manchester (061 [0161] 740 9438)
Preston College, Lancashire (0772 [01772] 254145)
Red Tape Studios, Sheffield (0742 7 [0114 2] 61151)
Sandwell Audio College, Sheffield (0742 7 [0114 2] 61131)
School Of Sound Recording, Manchester (061 [0161] 228 1830)
University College Salford, Manchester (061 [0161] 834 6633)

SCOTLAND

Clydebank College, Dumbartonshire (041 [0141] 952 7771, ex 216)
Jewel & Esk Valley College, Edinburgh (031 [0131] 669 8461, ex 235)
Stow College, Glasgow (041 [0141] 332 1786, ex 1026)

Hands-on experience at Manchester's School of Sound Recording

GENERAL INFORMATION

Music Consortium, Scotland (0738 [01738] 630802)) – advice on Scottish courses

Pop Goes To College (081 [0181] 332 6303) – book of UK music courses

UCAS (formerly UCCA/PCAS) (0242 [01242] 227788) – universities admissions service

Paul Quinn

DEMOS

No doubt about it: this is where we could get into a really interesting discussion about the whole subject of how you get from being A Muso to being A Star Muso. But the fundamental point is that, whether you're looking for gigs, a manager, or a record deal, you'll almost certainly find that a decent demo comes in handy at some stage along the way.

Whoever your demo may be aimed at, there is one convention that (in my opinion) you break at your peril – the 'three song rule'. The thinking here is that three tracks are enough to demonstrate that you're not just a one-song wonder, but not so many as to break the old show-biz saying: 'Always leave the audience wanting more'. (Look at it another way: if someone does show interest in your demo, you want to have something more to develop their enthusiasm.)

As to what three songs to use, I think the relevant point is that, with the exception of a few indie labels, the music biz is 5 percent music and 95 percent biz, and your choice of material – even the order in which you present the tracks – should reflect this. Put what you think is your most commercial song first, and your next-most commercial track last. The middle song could be one that illustrates some variation in your style; the classic example is a slow number. (Having raised the subjects of style and variation, I think it's worth mentioning a problem that quite a few musos encounter: where their music covers several different styles or genres, and they're tempted to put together a demo that demonstrates this versatility. With the possible exception of applying to be resident band at a Butlins, you should avoid this like the plague – it's a simple fact that the industry works by categorising/pigeon-holing/stereotyping just about every act that comes along, and if you and your music don't tell them what label you want to wear, they sure aren't going to bother figuring it out for you.)

Once you know what you're going to record, the obvious question is where to record it. If you've got your own 'serious' set-up, then that's clearly what you should use, but if you've only got a four-track and basics, you might want to consider using a pro studio. You'll find lots of thoughts on this in the *Commercial Studios* chapter, but the most important aspect *vis-à-vis* demos is that, though you should certainly expect a pro studio to deliver a better-sounding result, it could take you a long time (and therefore a lorra lolly) to achieve that result.

THE DEMO PACKAGE

We'll take the fairly frequent example of a band/solo artist sending a demo to a record company or, more likely, a whole batch of record companies. The first thing is to address your demo to someone by name – just putting 'A&R Dept' is a pretty effective way of saying: 'We're not serious'. With biggy labels you want the name of the head of A&R, with small labels you should probably be writing direct to the boss-person (you can get this info, and loadsa general advice, in *Making Music*'s A & R List).

Consider sending your demo to magazines that review them (such as *MM*'s Demology) – record industry people *do* read the reviews, and *have* been known to contact bands as a result. Some radio DJs, such as Radio 1's John Peel and GLR's Gary Crowley, also have a reputation not only for listening to demo tapes sent to them 'cold', but also for playing a chosen few on air.

There are five main items in your package: the demo tape, a photo of the guilty parties, a musical biography, a brief covering letter, and the actual package you put them all into. The tape itself should be something like TDK D with Dolby B – resist the urge to show off with chrome, metal or even, as I've heard some people do, DAT (your target might just want to play it on a car stereo or Walkman). If the tape has been used before, erase it first (I've actually heard demos where the last track runs straight into whatever was recorded previously). Start the first track about eight seconds in (three past the 'leader'), and leave a four second gap between tracks (enabling a listener with a 'music-search' player to skip or, hopefully, repeat a track). Rewind the tape, and knock out the record-protect tab. Label the cassette with your name, phone number, and track titles; repeat all of this, plus your address, on the inside of the inlay card.

At which point, we get to the little matter of what (if anything) to put on the front of the inlay in the way of artwork. This opens the door on the whole area of visual imaging, and what needs saying right now is that this is potentially very important, especially if your accompanying package doesn't include any decent visuals. At the very least, you want your outer package to say: 'Open me', and the contents to say: 'Play me.' If you have an artistic bent, and ideas on the image you want to project, you should still think carefully; on the one hand, your artwork may achieve the 'open me, play me' objectives; on the other, you're dealing with people who see *professional* artwork every day – can you cut it in such company?

If not, or if you simply don't have any arty inclinations, then you have two choices in terms of inlay visuals – stick to a plain inlay with text only, or get outside help. Professional help might be nice, but it might just break the bank as well. The alternative, which I strongly recommend, is to get friendly with one or more of the students at your local art college. These people are (one hopes) as keen about art as you're keen about music, and they're almost certainly full of ideas – in fact, the problem may not be in getting them interested, but in getting them to develop and project *your*

Package sent out by fetish band Mano Destra with demo tapes comprises professional studio portrait of singer Sarah Everitt (centre), photocopies of recent press coverage, and clear, concise, one-page, word-processed biog with Macintosh-designed letterhead

image, rather than whatever visual ideas currently turn them on. Ideally, you want a complete visual package that includes details like how your biography is laid out – at the least, you need a single 'logo' image, almost certainly based on your name, that you can plaster on package, photo (front or back), biog, letter and tape.

Ah yes, the photo. If you get an art student involved in your imaging, then this should be no problem. But if not, well, you'll find some advice in the aforementioned *Making Music* A & R List, the one subject it doesn't mention being who should shoot the pix. In the past I've recommended approaching local camera clubs – this could work fine if you know what you want, because photo-club members are generally on the lookout for new subjects, but you may not be dealing with, shall we say, quite the cutting edge of creativity... An alternative is to cobble together some kind of story for your local newspaper – they'll shoot their own pix, and though the result may very possibly make you look like a group of undertakers, the mere fact that it's 'in print' gives it credibility.

Your musical biography could take a number of forms – I've seen 'job-application' CV-style summaries through to colourised montages assembled from local press coverage. I don't think there's a single 'right' approach here, but I do think there are a few general rules. The presentation should look professional, and be easy to read and concise – avoid over-elaborate typography and remember that no one wants to know the ins and outs of every line-up change since you left primary school. Also, you really should avoid going over-the-top when describing the merits of your music and your achievements to date – self-confidence is one thing, arrant bull is another. End, if you can, with a schedule of forthcoming gigs.

The covering letter is where you get to say: 'I mean business'. In fact, this is pretty much all the letter is there for (except for contact details and perhaps repeating the upcoming gig dates). It's a biz letter, so arguably another area where you follow convention (like limiting the content of your tape to three songs). By all means get some paper printed with your logo, but if you don't know how to write the letter under the logo, check with your local librarian or maybe use a secretarial service gleaned from *Yellow Pages* .

Every item you send should have your name and (at least) phone number on it – the various bits may well get separated. If there are only certain times when you can be reached by phone, always print them wherever you put the number. I've already mentioned creating a package that says 'Open me' – it's just as important that your package be practical when somebody *does* decide to open it. I've handled demos where vital information was on scraps of paper that stayed buried when I shook the rest of the envelope out, while some offerings have been so securely wrapped and sealed that opening them took longer than listening to them.

Now that I've given you this wodge of sensible, down-to-earth advice, feel free to stuff these suggestions completely, if you feel that a more off-the-wall approach might work better for you. It certainly did for one band I know, who bombarded the *teenage daughter* of an A&R guy with their demos; she loved them, he signed them. Note, though, that this kind of stunt can backfire; he might just as likely have objected to a randy rocker pestering his virginal princess, and sent a couple of distressingly large friends round to discuss the difference between Iron Maiden and iron lung.

Above all, try to remember that, while you have your hopes, dreams and ambitions, industry people have their lunch breaks (he said deeply and cynically) – in addition to talent, you need determination, patience, and luck.

SOUND-PROOFING & ACOUSTICS

Independent producer Tony Lowe ponders a mix in the studio he built in his spare room

What we have here are two rather large topics, about which entire books could be written – and have been. A home recording manual is not really the appropriate place to look for a detailed analysis of the architectural and structural engineering problems inherent in studio construction, but at least I can try to give you a useful overview of what's involved.

SOUND-PROOFING

There are two basic aspects to sound-proofing: keeping unwanted external noise out, and keeping wanted sound in. The two often go hand-in-hand, and what we want in both cases is isolation. We can easily measure how much isolation we need by reference to the sound levels inside and outside a studio. Let's take a couple of examples: you want to record miked electric guitar at peak levels of around 100dBA, while your neighbours expect rural peace and tranquility, which is about 30dBA – so you need 70dB of isolation. Alternatively, your studio is overlooking a busy road (90dBA), and you want a really quiet environment (20dBA) – again, 70dB of isolation. These situations are not uncommon, and 70dB often crops up in the building specs for pro studios (you may argue that yours isn't 'true pro', but your neighbours, and the local council, may not be impressed by this argument). 70dB of isolation is by no means impossible, but that's a long way from saying that it's cheap, easy or convenient. Let's look at the problems...

Sound consists of variations in the pressure or density of the air that surrounds us. Imagine a speaker cone moving forward and backward – as it moves forward, it increases the air pressure, and when the high-pressure 'ridge' reaches, say, a wall, some of the pressure is reflected (creating echo), while some is absorbed. The absorbed energy tries to make the wall itself vibrate (like a giant loudspeaker cone), and this produces sound in the room next-door. What we're dealing with here is known as 'structure-borne' noise, and it's this, rather than the more obvious case of 'air-borne' noise, that is usually the cause of major problems.

There are three routes to attacking structure-borne noise: reduce the amount of sound energy reaching the walls/floor/ceiling, increase the mass of the walls etc (which means they will need higher sound levels before they start vibrating), and finally, when all else fails, build an isolated room-within-a-room.

You can cut the sound reaching a wall by using panels of acoustic strawboard, but the improvement is not all that great – nowhere near enough to solve serious problems like a need for 70dB of isolation. Increasing the mass of walls and such can produce isolation of maybe 50dB, and though this is jolly useful if you're building an extension, it's not generally a practical option.

Building a room-within-a-room isn't always practical either, but it is the best approach to serious noise-pollution problems. The basic walls, ceiling and floor of such a studio are fairly straightforward, but then we come to items like doors, windows, and a little number called the suspension. A double-door is virtually essential, but only works if both of the door panels are solid and a really good fit. Windows will definitely need to be double-glazed, but ordinary double-glazing is unlikely to be good enough – if you're heading for 70dB territory, you need something like one sheet of quarter-inch glass and one half-inch (seriously), with a spacing between them of at least six

Top: early stages in the construction of Tony Lowe's home studio...
Top left: the start of inner wall construction around the window area. Behind the inner panels is Rockwool infill, held in place with chickenwire.
Top right: Rockwool covers one entire wall while the adjoining wall awaits treatment. This picture also shows the timber frame on which the inner walls and false floor would later be mounted. The floor timbers are themselves mounted on one-inch plugs of industrial rubber.
Left: detail of the completed studio showing acoustic tiling of inner wall and Rockwool-filled, acoustic-tiled inner door The studio was designed in 1988 by Martin Deniz, using a scaled-down version of a specification found in a BBC handbook. Materials costs were about £1000 at 1988 prices; Martin and Tony did all the building work themselves...

inches. This is strictly custom-made territory, and even a moderately-sized window could set you back the best part of a grand.

And then there's the suspension. This involves mounting the whole caboodle on giant rubber bungs, which act like springs. This is not the kind of stuff you can pick up at B&Q, and there's a fair bit of calculating involved in planning such a structure (or you can end up with goodies like massive bass rumble, or a studio that 'wallows' about like a ship in a storm). There's also the marginally vital matter of your existing floor's ability to bear the extra weight, which could be a real problem with suspended wooden flooring. Beyond a shadow of a doubt, you need an experienced professional to plan and design the whole thing for you. A few of these people advertise in the music mags, but you'll find more if you check out industry books like *Showcase* (formerly *Kemps*) at your local reference library (though many specialists will only be interested in projects with a true pro budget).

Speaking of budgets, it's only natural that you'd like some idea of the possible total costs. This is well-nigh impossible, because circumstances vary wildly – but, plucking numbers from thin air, I doubt if you'd get design, construction materials, windows and such, for much under three grand, and even this assumes that you're going to provide most of the labour yourself. Clearly, many musos will simply stop reading at this point, but equally, if you consider that a decent 16-track set-up (with mikes, effects, DAT mastering and monitoring), is likely to set you back £10,000-plus, it doesn't actually seem ludicrous.

So far, we've been assuming that your problems are fairly serious. There are lots of cases where less drastic measures will fit the bill, but unless you're totally sure of what you're doing, I would still recommend bringing in a pro to advise you. For example, there's not much point spending money on a double-glazed window, if noise is still going to leak in through airbricks under a wooden floor (and you can't just seal up the airbricks, because then you're inviting rot).

ACOUSTICS

If the news on sound-proofing is largely both bad and expensive, the news on acoustics is generally both better and cheaper.

A lot of acoustics is about reverberation, and you'll find the basics on this in *Effects* – the other item we need to consider is resonance. Every object has at least one resonant frequency (which is where a sound at the frequency in question seems greatly amplified compared with other frequencies), and in the case of a simple box-shaped room, there are three such frequencies, determined by the length, width and height (and collectively known as the room 'eigentones') – these will be at bass frequencies, typically in the range 25-70hz. In many cases, this is not something you need to know much about, but in others there can be serious implications. Problems start where two dimensions of a room are identical or very similar, because you're then getting two loads of resonant 'boost' at the same frequency, and things are even worse with a cube-shaped room, where all three resonances coincide. These resonances can create 'boom' problems, both when miking up and when monitoring on speakers, and in most cases, there really isn't much you can do about them, short of calling in a professional to custom-design one or more 'bass traps'.

Back to room reverberation, where the obvious points are both quantity and quality (tonal character) in the room you're using. Perhaps surprisingly, the average living room or spare bedroom is generally quite acceptable. For miked recording, some pros might consider it a touch 'dead', but then others might judge it a tad lively, the apparent contradiction reflecting just how much recording practice is a matter of taste, rather than right or wrong. A room's suitability for monitoring is less easy to guess (partly because of the resonance/eigentone business mentioned above), but it's probably true to say that most home studios are rather on the lively side.

If you've got a large enough room, you could create 'live' and 'dead' ends, leaving bare walls and floor for the live part, and using heavy carpets and furnishings for the monitoring end. A very practical alternative for smaller rooms, or indeed larger rooms if you've got the dosh, is to keep the basic layout fairly lively, but have heavy floor-to-ceiling curtains that can be selectively drawn to deaden the acoustics.

Certain materials crop up time and again in any discussion of home studio acoustics: ceiling tiles, wall carpeting and egg-boxes. Ordinary ceiling tiles are largely irrelevant in modifying acoustics, but proper acoustic tiles can reduce 'brightness' (about £12 a square metre). Carpeting one or more walls will definitely deaden proceedings, but isn't usually necessary – heavy curtains, though probably more expensive than 'ex-exhibition' carpeting, are generally an adequate and less dramatic solution, plus of course, they're more flexible. Egg-boxes, which have featured in private studios for many, many years, do have an effect on acoustics, but not at all what many people hope for. They act as a 'diffuser' at mid-high frequencies, which cuts hard, bright echoes, but have no effect at all on problems like 'boom' (egg-boxes are also an appalling fire risk). Acoustic wall tiles will drastically deaden overall acoustics, but we're talking about £35 a square metre (that's around £800 to treat half a 15 x 12ft room).